HOW A Side Hustle CAN CHANGE YOUR LIFE

WHAT IF IT DOES WORK OUT?

Susie Moore

ixia
PRESS

Mineola, New York

Bibliographical Note

What If It DOES Work Out? How a Side Hustle Can Change Your Life
is a new work, first published by Ixia Press in 2017.

Library of Congress Cataloging-in-Publication Data

Names: Moore, Susie, author.
Title: What if it does work out? : how a side hustle can change your life /
Susie Moore.
Description: Mineola, New York : Ixia Press, 2017. | Includes bibliographical
references and index.
Identifiers: LCCN 2017021573| ISBN 9780486816494 (alk. paper) | ISBN
0486816494 (alk. paper)
Subjects: LCSH: Supplementary employment. | Part-time self-employment. | New
business enterprises. | Entrepreneurship.
Classification: LCC HD5854.5 .M66 2017 | DDC 658.1/1—dc23
LC record available at https://lccn.loc.gov/2017021573

IXIA PRESS
An imprint of Dover Publications, Inc.

Manufactured in the United States by LSC Communications
81649401   2017
www.doverpublications.com/ixiapress

CONTENTS

"Remember, becoming an entrepreneur early in life is one of the hallmarks of the most successful individuals throughout modern history."

–Jack Canfield

"How dare you settle for less when the world has made it so easy for you to be remarkable?"

–Seth Godin, author

"What is your passion? What stirs your soul and makes you feel like you're totally in harmony with why you showed up here in the first place? Know this for certain: Whatever it may be, you can make a living doing it and simultaneously provide a service for others. I guarantee it."

–Dr. Wayne W. Dyer

1

Why Wait?

"You don't have a career, you have a life."
–Cheryl Strayed, writer

*"Happiness is the joy that you feel when you are
moving towards your potential."*
–Shawn Achor, author and speaker

"Is this all there is?" I contemplated one morning while feeling restless at work. I was a sales director in New York for a Silicon Valley startup recently acquired by a Fortune 500 company. I was on a conference call in my freezing office, doused in artificial light, scouring Pinterest. I gazed through the window at the beautiful blue sky outside. Sigh. Then I saw a pin that struck me: a quote from poet Mary Oliver, from "The Summer Day":

*"Tell me, what is it you plan to do
with your one wild and precious life?"*

My soul screamed: "Not only this!"

It was time for change. And so it began. My side hustle. Does this sound like you, too? Maybe you are sitting in your air-conditioned boardroom, stuck in another mind-numbing internal meeting where the biggest egos just *love* to consume another hour of your life that you won't get back. Perhaps you are waiting for your (bad) drip coffee at 8:45 a.m. on a Tuesday, just aching to make it to Friday at 5 p.m. (Really, how can time pass so slowly?) Whatever your defining moment or moments are to you, you know it when you feel them.

For many, like tech founder Sean Behr, the impetus for creating a side hustle is dissatisfaction with their existing day job. As Sean says about the time before launching his company Stratim, "I wasn't creating anything new. As an entrepreneur I've always wanted to create—new ideas, new products, new companies."

In my case, after more than a decade in sales (which in large part, I loved) I felt ready for something new. I also know that as human beings we are wired for new challenges and experiences. And I'm not alone: a 2013 Gallup survey showed that only 13 percent of employees worldwide are engaged at work.

I've read more than 550 personal development books and I am a natural adviser to the people in my life, especially when it comes to connecting them to their purpose, becoming more confident, negotiating, and networking. My side hustle, naturally, became life coaching.

I joined New York University's coaching program and used my sales skills to pitch article ideas to editors. I wanted to get my work published so I could attract clients. (It's called a hustle for a reason!) You may find that certification isn't necessary for the field you want to break into, in which case you can dive right in.

In my case, my advice-based articles helped generate a string of clients and within a couple of months I was earning money both writing and coaching. I couldn't believe my luck! Getting paid to talk to people and give life advice? There is a God! While writing for *Marie Claire* I even got to interview some pretty incredible people, including Arianna Huffington, Kris Jenner, and Spanx founder Sara Blakely.

Writing earned me between $75 and $750 per article (from the publications that paid) and I wrote multiple pieces a month. I was typing away everywhere: on the subway, in the Whole Foods line, while on a lunch break at the office. Each piece took two to three hours to complete. Writing for major publications with tens of millions of monthly unique visitors not only gave me credibility, it drove traffic to my blog—resulting in additional email subscribers who in turn often sought coaching or advice from me.

I started coaching people at $100 a session in my very first or second week of taking classes and, as demand increased (largely due to my content being shared on social media) and as my life-coaching skills developed, I was able to raise my prices every three months or so in $50 increments. Working around the commitments of my day job, which included travel and after-hours client entertainment, some months I made an extra $4,000 on my side hustle. That was working 12 to 16 hours a week on top of my day job. According to Nielsen, the average 35- to 49-year-old American watches more than 33 hours of television a week. You do the math.

What could you do with those extra hours each week? Think about that for a second. If you sacrifice some weekly screen time, or give up or reduce any other unproductive habit, what gains could you create in your well-being or your goals? What could an extra income from hustling in those hours do for your life?

I could not recommend side hustling more highly. You make extra money, use talents that lie dormant in your nine-to-five day job—and hedge your bets against an uncertain economy. Starting a business while employed also allows you to determine proof of concept more safely by providing for a test run that indicates your side hustle's viability. This means you can prove that your product or service is wanted in the world before you dedicate your full-time focus towards it.

But it's not always a breeze. You will need a combination of creative thinking and hard work to attract your first clients and build your brand. Add onto that the need to manage cash flow, handle various administrative tasks (including outsourcing as appropriate), *and* look for ways to make these more efficient so your hustle can scale.

You need to be committed for this. You will have to forgo that *Game of Thrones* binge session you planned and you will often be first to leave the bar. You will have to overcome self-doubt about charging for work that a lot of the time feels like fun. "No" will be your new favorite word. BUT the payoff can be incredible. After almost 18 months of juggling my rapidly expanding hustle, I resigned from my full-time job. This was no mean feat, as my job, in that final year, grossed around $500,000. That is how much I loved my new life-coaching gig and trusted in my hustle's expansion.

Did people think I was nuts? Yes! Heck—*I* even thought I might be nuts. But, long-term, it didn't seem that risky really. Think about it. There is no security in the employment market. I, like anyone else, could be fired (based on a single person's decision!) at any time. I considered the value of freedom over my schedule, doing work that I cared about, and losing my income ceiling (especially as a woman—I felt I'd hit it) worth the downside of financial risk from ditching a consistent paycheck. After all, I also got to leave behind an unpredictable boss and the stress and pressure of continuing to do work that I had begun to resent. And I grew up in a household with no money—we were on welfare, in fact—so I respect money and do not take financial risk lightly. Consider if you are weighing the risks too highly, and whether you can't shift your perspective.

To help you make the plunge, at the end of each chapter you'll find a call to action to help you apply the principles I discuss. Homework, if you like. I hope these will keep you motivated as you read this book. I have also interspersed some advice from a range of badass entrepreneurs and people who've started very successful side hustles. I hope you enjoy them and learn something from them too.

I bet you're a lot like me; you just want freedom in your life and ownership of your work. We all want to make a meaningful impact in the world doing work that we love. On our own terms. The rest of this book will encourage you to take the leap of believing in yourself, examine what's holding you back, and push you to step up to the plate and knock it out of the park.

To hustlers everywhere—you're not alone. This is for you: a

road map for how to strike out into the unknown of your passion project and take your success into your own hands.

Over to you ✦ ✦ ✦ ✦ ✦ ✦ ✦ ✦

When you're stuck on a conference call or dealing with corporate red tape or stressed out by your day job, what's the escape hatch you dream about? Create an inventory of your personal strengths and your pie-in-the-sky job list. What would *your* ideal side hustle be? You can start by asking yourself these questions!

✦ What problems do I help people solve?

✦ What makes me feel alive?

✦ What would I do if money were no object?

If you need a little help, ask a friend or loved one what you are good at, or something that you have helped them with. Be open to receive their feedback. The answers might just surprise (and totally delight) you—and if you listen closely, they might reveal a new path to follow!

2

Getting Over Fear (It's Possible)

"Fear kills more dreams than failure ever will."
–Suzy Kassem, writer, poet, philosopher

"Our doubts are traitors, and make us lose the good we oft might win, by fearing to attempt."
–William Shakespeare, *Measure for Measure*

"Susie, the general manager would like to see you." My heart seized in my chest. "This is *it!*" I thought to myself. I was getting promoted!

I was young, naïve, and ambitious (not to mention a little cocky) when I started out in my career. I joined my first company in an entry-level support role and I was desperate to get into sales. I spent all my time with the sales team, listening to them, helping them with their clients, upselling whenever I had the chance.

"They *have* to be noticing this great work!" I kept thinking rather confidently to myself while totally ignoring the data entry I was supposed to be doing.

So when the big boss wanted to see me, I was ready. I threw on a dab of lip gloss and strutted up those stairs, prepared to gracefully accept my promotion. Oh, and I was gonna request business cards too (in my mind, business cards meant that you had hit the BIG time).

Instead, as soon as my butt hit the chair these words slapped me in the face: "Susie, we're letting you go. It's not working out."

Full-body shock. My breathing stopped. My heart sank. *Whaaaaat?!?!*

I was in my early twenties, living in Australia with little money and no family to turn to (they were back in the U.K. where I grew up). But I found an inner strength that stirred in times like these. Our internal guidance never fails us when we allow it to rise. It told me what I needed to do. I needed to make a bold move—get up, get out, and start over. Immediately.

I wish I could revisit that sad, scared girl that afternoon and tell her that everything turns out OK. Much better than OK, even.

Was the fear of being twenty-three, alone in a new country with little cash—and now unemployed!—just in my mind? Hell no! I was terrified. The fear was real. Fear is always real. Fear of change is one of the biggest preventers for our changing anything in our lives at all.

I'm not here to diminish fear. I feel like I could write 300 books on the subject. It makes an appearance in almost every single blog post I have ever written. Fear manifests itself in a million ugly ways. It shows up as excuses. Or procrastination. It shows up as practicality: "Oh, I'd love to be a photographer but I can't make money that way." It shows up as confusion or ignorance: "I have no idea what my purpose is."

As a life coach, I find the trickiest part of getting to the core of what someone wants is having them say out loud what they really, really want. Not to me, **but to themselves.** Once we say it aloud it has a certain power. Many dreams are buried because we are too scared to voice them to ourselves. When we speak them, dreams become real. And that's terrifying because we know what we need to do.

It may not seem obvious at first but, more often than not, if something scares us it's because it's important to us. It's shining a light on something that matters so deeply to our being that it CAN scare us. Because it has the ability to. One of my friends with a stunning voice has a secret dream of being a singer. But she laughs it off, plays it down, and only allows the very existence of this long-buried dream to appear after a few sauvignon blancs. Why? Because she's afraid of what she'll have to do if she realizes it. I mean, what if she says aloud, "I'm a singer. I want to sing. I want people to hear me"? It's far easier for her to pretend that it doesn't exist. Because if she made it real by saying it, what then?

But once we understand fear, we can stop being at its mercy. So here is the skinny on fear.

According to Dan Baker, Ph.D., and Cameron Stauth, authors of *What Happy People Know*, unless your fear is the protective force that stops you from doing something dangerous (like hitching a ride with a total stranger, for example) all fears belong to two groups. Yes, just two groups!

All fears can be attributed to a belief in the following:

1. **I AM NOT ENOUGH**

2. **I DO NOT HAVE ENOUGH**

As humans we have not evolved to take into account our new modern surroundings. Back in the day of the caveman these fears were real and the result of their being actualized was certain death. If you were not fit, healthy, and strong, the tribe would leave you behind in order to survive. And if you did not have enough—meaning if you did not collect food every day and have the materials to give you shelter and warmth—you would perish.

And today?

Being "enough" in today's world means being educated, connected, charming, smart, good-looking, thin, interesting . . . the list is endless, especially when you are busy comparing yourself to your peers.

Having "enough" in our society means possessing the luxuries that we see touted as equaling success but that can also trap us: a large home, fancy car, great wardrobe. It requires dropping cash we may not even have on stuff we don't need to try and keep up with our friends.

The circumstances are very different but the two innate, "reptilian brain" fears remain. Observe any fear that is strong or subtle in your life and you will be able to attribute it to one of these two fear groups.

These are all examples of **I AM NOT ENOUGH**:

✦ *"I can't tell that person I like them;*
   he or she won't possibly be attracted to me!"

✦ *"I can't ask for more money at work.*
   It's not like I'm perfect at my job."

✦ *"Who am I to start a business?"*

✦ *"I can't start a blog—*
   no one wants to hear what I have to say."

✦ *"I don't want to go to that party.*
   I'm not good with new people."

Sound familiar?

What about these:

✦ *"Money is hard to come by."*

✦ *"John comes from a better family than I do . . . I'm*
   kinda embarrassed to introduce him to my parents."

✦ *"Better to stick to the career I know than take a risk*
   doing what I really would love to do and go broke."

✦ *"Tom makes a lot more money than I do and always has nice things. I feel like he's better than me."*

✦ *"I won't buy those boots/that laptop/a gym membership—I hate parting with money."*

They are all examples of **I DO NOT HAVE ENOUGH**.

Not all of these examples will come down to fear for everyone. Perhaps you are more of an introvert than a partygoer. Maybe you would rather save for a vacation or a down payment on an apartment than go shopping for clothes. But only YOU know the true motivation behind statements you make or think. If your soul is stirred with a reason for not doing something that feels right and fair, great. If not—if your decisions leave you feeling insecure, small, and unsatisfied—fear has got you wrapped around its little finger, my friend. For my friend the singer, her fear keeps her dissatisfied, not empowered. She stays put to avoid having to feel vulnerable, exposed, and then in a position to have to do some work. Real work using a real gift that has the potential to bring real joy. But as my friend, best-selling author James Altucher, says, "Rejection and the fear of rejection is the biggest impediment we face to choosing ourselves." My singer friend, like many of us, won't even make that rejection (or its opposite, success) possible.

In some cases this may express itself as doing things for the wrong reasons, motivated by external opinion and "shoulds" that desire external approval above all else. Aaron Clausen, a client of mine who is the CEO of an app called NatureMapr, has insight on this from his own mistakes:

"Another lesson I learned the hard way was trying to build or design a business based on where I thought there was an obvious gap and/or opportunity in the market. But what I found was that nobody cared about what I was doing. It was so hard to get any help or interest. News flash: I was in fact doing it for the wrong reasons. I had started that business to 'try to be successful.' It was four years of huge slog, the hardest I've ever worked in my life, and I was only lucky to be able to get out by offloading it to a much larger fish in the pond. I wouldn't recommend that approach. The funny thing about NatureMapr is that when I hit rock bottom after much business and career stress I just started going mountain biking, bush walking, and wandering out-doors to escape all my stresses as a way to kind of meditate and chill out. And it was exactly there, where I loved what I was doing, that my next business found me. I definitely didn't force it and it just happened on its own. Don't force it, do what you love."

Often we avoid this introspection. We just want to fit in. We want other people to like and respect us. Our self-esteem is built on what other people value, even when that is not necessarily what we really want. We are afraid to be different, but the funny thing is, what makes us different is what makes us interesting. It makes us beautiful, noticeable, and uniquely useful in the world. Consider your favorite singer, author, actor, entrepreneur—anyone who has inspired you. I bet you your life savings they were misfits or described as people who go against the grain. Look at Madonna. Amy Schumer. Steve Jobs. David Bowie. Whatever you think of these people, it can't be denied that they don't blend in. My friend Alex Cavoulacos, co-founder of career site The Muse, tapped into this when she told me one of her guidelines for success is as simple as this: "Be yourself."

Investment guru James Altucher had his own realization that he needed to march to the beat of his own drum. What he shared with me may help inspire you to do the same:

"From an early age I was taught to obey the rules of society. Rules that were put there largely for good reasons: it's good to stop at stop signs so you don't hurt anyone; it's good to get an education so you can get a job; it's good to own a home so you can have roots and build value while your kids have a consistent place to play.

"We've been taught by parents, teachers, bosses—even friends—what is 'good' for us. We are also taught by trillions of dollars in marketing what is 'good' for us. A 15-trillion-dollar mortgage industry. A trillion-dollar student loan industry (education is good!), the trillion-dollar economy that needs workers to blindly put fuel into its engines.

"This is all fine. But we are not standardized widgets inside a giant robot. Ultimately, we are unique people who have lives to live. We have to develop our own rules that we will adhere to. Rules that will give us well-being, happiness, and success.

"If we don't come up with our own guidelines of what will make us happy, then who will? Well, we know the answer: Everyone else will. And it is a guarantee it will not be in our best interests. Not that everyone else is trying to hurt us. It's just that only we know what will be best for us. And often, knowing what will be best for me is something I had to learn through a lot of trial and error while experimenting with the rules and guidelines of others."

So: what are *your* rules? How can you stop listening to fears and judgments around what you "should" do in order to do what you know you must, no matter anyone's opinion?

Over to you ✦ ✦ ✦ ✦ ✦ ✦ ✦ ✦

- ✦ Think of two instances where fear has prevented you from doing something that might have been harmful. What was the outcome? You can be grateful to your fear for this.

- ✦ Think of three times in your life where you were afraid to do something that you didn't feel ready to do but found the courage and pushed through anyway. What were the positive things that came out of each of these three experiences?

- ✦ Consider one big, current fear. Identify whether it is a harmful fear or an ego-based fear—having enough or being enough. If it is

a legitimate fear—something that will result
in serious harm—thank your fear for keeping
you safe. If it is the more likely fear there only
to protect your ego from risk, you can say,
"Thanks, fear. I can take it from here."

Consider how you can view your current fear as an opportunity to learn, grow, and unearth more of your inner power. That feeling stirring within you is something good waiting to happen. Your fear is actually showing you what you need to do next. After all, the sensation is often no different from excitement once we reframe it. We'll deal with ways to move past that fear in the next chapter, but for now, let's pause to respect and honor our fear as a vital and necessary part of our growth. Think of five times you were afraid of an event (maybe public speaking, asking for a raise, confronting a friend or relative about something) and after the event you realized you didn't have to worry so much.

How did things work out?

Are you glad you did it?

What does this reveal to you about what you can do next?

3

How Can I Get Past My Fear?

*"I want us all liberated from the path of fear,
for many reasons—but mostly because it
makes for such a damn boring life.
Fear only ever tells you one thing: STOP.
Whereas creativity, courage, and inspiration
only ever want you to GO."*

—Elizabeth Gilbert, author

*"Most fear is just bad management of our
own mental faculties."*

—Brendon Burchard, motivational author

My hands were sweating. My heart was beating. I looked in the mirror and asked myself, "Why do you always do such crazy shit?" I was not about to jump off a cliff. Nor was I about to do anything illegal. I was about to interview self-made billionaire Sara Blakely, the founder of Spanx, for *Marie Claire*.

To me, *Marie Claire* has always been one of the coolest publications in the world (even when I was younger and could never afford it). I am not a journalist. I did not go to journalism school. I did not even graduate from college. But somehow with a lot of time, persistence, and effort, I managed to secure an interview with one of the world's most successful women for one of the world's most credible publishing houses. I was nervous, on edge, but I got on the phone and the interview happened. I had 42 minutes with one of the smartest businesspeople on the planet. How did it go?

Beautifully. I got lost in what she was saying. I felt like we were old friends. In fact, not only was Sara awesome and inspiring and funny and real, the article was popular and was published by her team on the Spanx homepage. She even sent me a bottle of champagne to say thanks.

Similar fears have risen within me on multiple occasions:

✦ When approaching my school principal about changing the unfair system for kids who had a free school lunch (I was one of them). We were forced to present a very obvious "my family is really poor" token to the lunch lady in front of all the other kids, which made us feel humiliated.

✦ Presenting to 20 or more people in boardrooms in New York and Washington, D.C., in my sales career.

✦ During a live television interview with a popular TV show in Australia, discussing how to ask for what you want.

✦ When I saw Jake Gyllenhaal in a downtown New York City restaurant and knew I had to introduce myself (he was lovely).

✦ Arriving in New York with no network, job opportunities, or work authorization and knowing I had to present like a boss in interviews to get the job.

✦ When I quit my lucrative corporate job. I had a plan and a lot of faith and a commitment to work my butt off. But it was still scary.

✦ Getting married for the second time. I knew it was right this time but still felt scared because of my first experience.

✦ When I also interviewed Kris Jenner and Kelly Osbourne, also for *Marie Claire*. They were both very candid and surprisingly cool.

The lesson? *You* are in the driver's seat of your life. Your fear is not. Fear will always accompany you, no matter how much you could pay a Park Avenue therapist to eradicate it. But your fears are not in control. You are.

A wonderful thing about life and growth is that the more you take on new challenges—when you let what is greater than fear, your desires, lead—your fear subsides. It has no choice, as there is nowhere for it to go but into the background. In the face of action, fear dissolves. This I know for sure. But fear will never evaporate from your life. It can't. I like to think of it this way: "If I had no fear in my life I would have nothing left to do here on earth, would I?"

Remember that at one point in your life you were afraid to have your first kiss. You were afraid to leave home. You were afraid on your first day of school and then your first day of work. But you moved forward anyway. The fear back then was the same as your fear today. The situations just keep getting bigger.

Fear's essence is to protect you. (Remember that pesky reptilian part of the brain that wants to keep you safe and away from new, potentially dangerous situations?) It pops up 99 percent of the time unrequired.

Your fear never has to rule. In large part it shows you what you need to do next. My friend Molly recently shared with me her two favorite sayings about fear: "It's not fair, but the way things work is that we get the courage to do the things that scare us shitless *after* we do them, not before"; and "Courage is not absence of fear but rather the judgment that something else is more important than fear." Jason Wachob, CEO of mindbodygreen, summed it up beautifully for me when explaining his ability to master fear of things not working out: "I had started and been part of early-stage startups that didn't work, so I knew that it wasn't the end of the world (if I failed). I also lost my father suddenly to a heart attack when I was just 19 years old. When you lose a parent when you're young, it's devastating but then you make it through it. Things like failure or rejection don't seem like a big deal when you've experienced that type of grief."

Think about this too. There exists a very overused saying: "believe in yourself." Sometimes this is hard, especially in manic moments of self-doubt. So when it comes to making your side hustle your reality you can switch to, "believe in your work." One overworked Thursday you might have had a bad day at the office and come home to an unhappy side hustle client (this will happen, and it's OK). You will feel low, drained, and sad and will ask yourself: Why am I doing all of this? You will want to give up, go to sleep or watch TV until your eyes are square. But it will pass and you will soon have a great day at the office, a beaming client, and more of a cash injection in your account than you imagined in a month.

In these moments, ask yourself what is most important to you: pursuing your dream, or letting a bad day (or series of bad days) bring it to an end? Becoming who you are meant to be, or waiting for some criticism from a frenemy that may never even arrive?

It's time to make it real.

What will you do today and by the end of the week that will bust through your side hustle blocks? Write that comedy script? Buy the URL for the food blog you've always dreamed of starting? Create an email contact list of who to inform that you're launching a matchmaking service, personal branding business, or life coaching practice?

Take a small step. Today. Give yourself two deadlines: one 24-hour deadline and one 7-day deadline to take two steps towards starting or building upon your side hustle.

"Whenever you have a problem, repeat over and over, 'All is well. Everything is working out for my highest good. Out of this situation only good will come and I am safe.' This simple affirmation will work miracles in your life."
–Louise Hay, motivational speaker, founder of Hay House

Before I launched my side hustle as a life coach and writer, I was depressed. Don't get me wrong, for a very long time I really loved my sales career. I was good at it. I made all my friendships working in advertising. It allowed me, and my husband, to have a very nice lifestyle. I had the most fun of my life traveling, meeting people, learning about cool and innovative online products. I was grateful for all of those things.

But I had learned and mastered everything I wanted to in that career. I did not want to be a senior vice president of sales. I did not want to sell other products in a different company ("same shit, different toilet," as my friend Tal jokes). I was ready to abandon what had become so familiar to me. My heart knew it. I felt my heart beating inside my chest and some days I even felt in pain when I could not see a transition in sight. Poet and philosopher Mark Nepo explains it really well. He says that life is a continuous cycle of "learning, mastery, and abandonment."

I knew there was something new for me to learn and master! After half-heartedly doing some interview training as a side business, I decided I needed to kick myself in the butt and get a legit side hustle going. I found the website of a New York City life coach and asked if I could take her to lunch to learn a bit about her business. I did the same with another coach. I loved meeting them. They opened up my eyes. Their work was really meaningful to them. And they did it full time! They ran their own schedule (freedom!) and helped people all day. I signed up at New York University as soon as enrollment began, and my life-coaching path began.

Around this time I turned thirty. This is an age that we refer to in coaching as when we transition out of "novice adulthood." That was exactly how I felt. It was time to get real about my life and my life's real work. I did not want a decade to pass and to still feel this way (or probably a lot worse). I had also gained weight. I was drinking a lot. I didn't realize it—it happened so slowly over time. Does any of this feel familiar? There are signs that something needs to change when you pay attention. What might you be missing? Are you losing enthusiasm to work out (or working out like crazy to overcompensate for your stress)? Are you turning down invitations out of exhaustion and withdrawal from the world (not to be confused with refusing in honor of self-care and protecting all-important "you time")? Do your friends notice a difference between you today and you a few years ago, back when you were full of vitality and a zest for living?

Once my side hustle was alive and kicking—and profitable—I felt a renewed passion for my life. For everything. I even kinda enjoyed my job again! I saw it as a placeholder for my "real career."

I saw everyone—clients, colleagues, peers—in a new, life-coaching light. I felt lighter (and became physically lighter). I started introducing myself as a life coach. My corporate clients and peers were psyched for me too! I blended the two worlds however I could. People even told me I looked good. It was a direct reflection of how I felt. Because I *felt* good.

For example, when the startup I helped build for almost four years was purchased by AOL, I realized AOL also owns *The Huffington Post*. So who did I email? Arianna Huffington! And what did she do? Not only was she extremely nice and complimentary of the writing sample I sent her, but she also got an editor to set me up as a contributor on their platform. And who is a prolific contributor in their healthy lifestyle section? Me! That might even be how you heard about me in the first place. Since then, I have interviewed her twice and she has personally shared my work on social media a couple of times.

There are two lessons here:

1. **You have to be resourceful.** Who do you know within your network (including a few degrees of separation) that could be a great connection for you on your entrepreneurial journey?

2. **Important people are more approachable than you realize.** Because people rarely approach them.

My "colleague" Arianna really hooked me up. There are opportunities everywhere if you open your eyes and look. Who might be a possible mentor? The side hustle really puts you in that positive, go-getting, magnetic zone. With a negative, closed attitude this massive opportunity would never have been seized. And it almost wasn't. As an example, a client of mine in Chicago was buzzing after spending a couple of hours in a borrowed studio making art. Her artistic side hustle made her feel renewed, refreshed, and alive. She was enjoying a lunch break at Soho House and struck up a conversation with a stranger at the bar (her energy that day was magnetic—the most beautiful side hustle side effect). Turns out he was an artist, too—with a thriving gallery. As "luck" would have it—they became friends. And they are now friends with (financial) benefits as she prepares to debut her work in his gallery. The truth bomb here is that the more you hustle (with heart!), the luckier you get. If she had spent that Saturday morning on Instagram this tête-à-tête would have remained a distant dream. Instead things started working out, as they have a tendency to do once you start believing in yourself.

So, let's get down to the nitty-gritty. We have to get over the fear of failure, fast. Alex Cavoulacos, co-founder of career website The Muse, said this about getting her business off the ground with her fellow founder Kathryn Minshew:

> "We were definitely scared of failure and faced a lot of rejection, day in and day out—and still do. What made it easier was thinking through the worst-case scenario: what if we gave it our all, tried and tried, but didn't make it work, got into debt, moved in with friends or family, and finally realized we had to pull the plug on our dream? Painful? Definitely. But not something we couldn't

recover from. If that happened, we'd have to take the first decently paying job we got, pay off our debts, and decide what we wanted to do next. Certainly not the outcome we wanted, but by thinking about how bad it could get we realized it was a risk we were willing to take. If the worst did happen, it still wouldn't be the end of the story."

These are probably the worst things you are thinking can happen when you launch your side hustle:

- ✦ You happen to lose some money in setup costs.
- ✦ You change your mind about your side hustle idea.
- ✦ People laugh when you tell them about it.
- ✦ You don't know what to do or how to start.
- ✦ You start and then quit.
- ✦ You never make any money from it.
- ✦ Your company/boss is not supportive.
- ✦ You find your passion disappointing.
- ✦ You aren't good at your side hustle.
- ✦ Someone says "I told you so."

Perhaps the worst that can happen is your side hustle builds, you quit your job to focus on it full time, and for whatever reason your new income flow is not financially sustainable. SO WHAT? If it does fail, most of the time you can get another job and then reassess. This is especially true if you keep your network alive! Keeping in touch with people is important and when you do, almost nothing in career-land is irreversible.

As my friend Sean Behr taught me, "The American game of baseball provides a great lesson in failure and rejection. The best baseball players in the world fail 70 percent of the time when hitting a baseball. When a baseball player fails there is no ongoing gloom; there is no long sense of failure—only another opportunity to hit in the future. I think that's a good analogy for those starting their own business."

What an awesome perspective! Remember that sometimes people lose their jobs without having a side hustle to fall back on. Additionally, they can leave one position and later find another if the new venture they left for comes to an end. Pursuing your hustle will make you feel more empowered and therefore more able to handle life's inevitable challenges with a far greater feeling of freedom along the way. I love what James Altucher says about fear and freedom:

"What I want most is *well-being*:

- ✦ Always improving my competence in something I love
- ✦ Always improving my connections with friends and the people I love

Always moving towards a sense of freedom. That feeling where no anxiety or stress can bring me down. A sense that I can make the decisions that are good for me and then act on them, whatever they are."

An Important Note about Impostor Syndrome

Here is one other thing you need to watch out for as you start your own journey to freedom: impostor syndrome. This is one of fear's sneakiest friends and the main culprit preventing anyone starting and making money from a side hustle or entrepreneurial venture. Be aware of this sneaky, ever-present drain on your confidence. Impostor syndrome is what we experience when we feel we don't deserve our accomplishments or question whether we are in any position to start a business. When we experience success we may feel we've fooled others into thinking we are capable and may attribute our achievements to blind luck or good timing. Our inability to accept our gifts means we feel like a fraud or an impostor—maybe even waiting to be exposed as undeserving of our success. This is why so many potentially beautiful side hustles never launch. We say, "Who am I to . . . "

Most common in high-achieving women, impostor syndrome not only prevents us from enjoying success, it also massively limits our potential. Feeling nondeserving and like a fake, we turn down wonderful new opportunities and creative ideas. Impostor syndrome is the killer of many "what-might-have-beens."

Does that sound like you? It sure sounds a lot like the excuses I hear all the time (including from myself on my bad days). People I coach always tell me they are "not ready" for the next step. Moving to a different city. Starting an entrepreneurial venture. Online dating. Applying for a role at a prestigious company. The truth is, we're never ready. But those who get what they want in this world proceed anyway. In the words of author Susan Jeffers, they "feel the fear and do it anyway." They know there is nothing to lose and a whole lot to gain by taking action. And the more you do it, the easier it becomes over time. It can also feel quite thrilling. I have never felt more alive than when I have moved to a new country, quit jobs, and launched entrepreneurial projects. So when you hear the voice in your head whisper that you're not talented or smart enough to succeed at your dreams, remember that it's only a thought in your head, not reality.

Then flip the fear and ask yourself: What is the best that can happen if I believe in my awesomeness and get started? I guess there is only one way to find out.

Over to you ✦ ✦ ✦ ✦ ✦ ✦ ✦ ✦ ✦

Write all your concerns down. But don't stop there. Keep asking yourself after each one: And then what? And then what? Keep writing. I promise it won't end up with you toothless, living under a bridge.

4

How to Find Your Side Hustle

"You have to love your side business because you'll be working on it at night, on the weekends, and in almost every spare hour you can find."
    –Kimberly Palmer, *The Economy of You*

"Solve big problems. Whether you are working for a company or starting a business, solve big problems. If you solve a problem for people, they will want to work with you, buy your product or service, and likely pay you for it."   –Sean Behr, tech founder

Some of the most successful side-giggers I interviewed built businesses that cost very little to start, could be scaled up easily as they grew, fit well with their full-time jobs, took advantage of their own passions and creativity, and most importantly, were incredibly enjoyable.

We've covered the benefits of a side hustle and they are endless: financial freedom, creative freedom, working on something that aligns with your passions, greater options if your day job goes sideways, and the thrill of setting your own agenda. But how do you know what business idea you should pursue?

There are a million things that can jolt you into starting a business. A lightbulb idea, dissatisfaction at work, an unexpected life event. For my friend Jason Wachob, author of *Wellth: How I Learned to Build a Life, Not a Résumé*, it was his health:

> "I was running another company and trying to raise capital when I discovered I had two extruded discs in my lower back pressing on my sciatic nerve. I could barely walk and almost had back surgery. Looking back, it was probably related to an old college basketball injury combined with stress and the fact that I was flying almost 100,000 miles a year. Being six foot seven and scrunched into airline seats didn't help. One doctor told me that yoga might be a way to avoid surgery. So I started practicing yoga daily, and was very surprised that I loved it. From there, I got interested in a more holistic lifestyle. I ate organic and ditched toxic household products. I began to meditate. I started a gratitude practice. And after just a few months, I completely healed my back (without surgery). It was a real awakening for me. I realized that health wasn't about weight loss or looking good—it was a blend of how we treated our minds, bodies, and the environment. It was also the inspiration for starting mindbodygreen."

Another friend of mine, Rupa Mehta, founder of the fitness company Nalini Method in New York, says about starting her business:

> "I was at a crossroads in my twenties, debating between moving back to my comforting hometown in Virginia or staying in New York, pursuing my adventurous side and passion. The thing that kept ringing in my ears was, 'Teach, teach, teach.' It was definitely a risky venture but I wanted something I could jump into with both feet, knowing I was following my heart. Nalini Method was built from the desire for a home base in a big city; a studio that clients could call 'home.' I knew I couldn't live without teaching in my life, so I built a business that combined my love of home, teaching, and fitness."

The key is to tap into your dreams, whatever they may be. Spreading the word about wellness, teaching—there are a million options out there. In fact, there has never been a better time in history to be an entrepreneur. Seth Godin calls being alive right now "the opportunity of a lifetime." He is right. But opportunities just sit there if you don't take advantage of them.

Here is my time-tested formula that I use with new clients who come to me, eager to start their own side gig but not sure where to start. It's called the Skill Distiller Formula.

The Three-Step Formula to Uncover Your Skills (That Will Pay the Bills!)

I created the *Skill Distiller Formula* to help my clients understand the strengths they already have inside of them. It will uncover the skills that will form the basis of your side hustle strategy using only three simple steps.

1. Think of three big problems you've solved or successes you've had.

These don't have to be work-related. And they don't have to be impressive by anyone else's standards. Just **brainstorm three things that you're proud to have achieved or three problems you're proud to have solved.**

Here are a few examples:

- ✦ I found and bought my dream house in one month, $25K under budget.
- ✦ I helped my best friend through a really difficult divorce.
- ✦ My sister was struggling to find employment and I helped her land a well-paying job that she loves.
- ✦ I graduated from college at the top of my class.
- ✦ I backpacked through Europe, completely on my own.

Once you have your list, you're ready for step 2.

2. Identify the skills that helped you achieve these three things.

I need you to step outside of yourself for a moment. Humble people (or those struggling with that pesky old impostor syndrome) find this step really difficult to do. If you're used to downplaying your accomplishments, you might look at your list and say, "*I didn't do anything all that special to achieve those results.*"

But you did. You have a set of strengths and skills that enabled you to do all three of those rad things you listed above. Not everyone could have done that, and *no one* could have done it in the same way that you did.

It's so rare that we take time to acknowledge all that we've done and all that we're capable of. But it's essential to recognize your strengths if you want to build a successful side hustle.

Let your mind explore everything you bring to the table that allowed you to achieve those accomplishments or solve those problems.

Let's keep going with an example from above. To help your sister find a job, you put your feelers out into your network. You asked friends who love their jobs for hiring advice. You connected the dots between the right contacts to find some great opportunities for your sister at fantastic companies.

Your attention to detail made a big difference in polishing up your sister's résumé. You helped your sister position herself as an asset to the companies so she would nail the interview. You also taught her how to follow up in a way that was assertive but never pushy.

In reflecting, you realize that you're amazing at engaging your community to help you reach your goals. You're comfortable asking questions, you're great at positioning, and you're excellent at utilizing good connections. These are all insanely valuable skills that will set the stage for a profitable side hustle, if you use them.

Or, in the case of the house purchase, you are comfortable doing the research and processing a lot of information to determine the relative value of real estate in your area. You also come to realize that you are a pretty good negotiator and cool under pressure, not allowing your emotions to get in the way of your judgment.

3. Think about how you can apply your skills in a new way.

Remember, a successful side hustle is all about doing the best you can with what you have. What you have is a clear set of skills that have already proven to get you results. So let's brainstorm how you can use them in the best way possible.

Maybe you want to start a knitting group where people pay you $100 for two hours to teach them how to knit on a Sunday.

How can you apply your skills to move the (knitting) needle forward?

Your openness to asking questions is going to be a huge strength in building your side hustle. Who could you ask for advice on starting a weekly group? Who's done something similar who can guide you? Who can point out the unexpected pitfalls to avoid?

You'll want to lean on your network and strong sense of community, too. Who can you invite to join the club? Who are the social butterflies with big circles that will spread the word quickly? Who knows somebody at *Creative Knitters* magazine that can run a feature on your new club? You had a way of making your friends *want* to connect your sister with their HR directors. How can you use that same mentality to incentivize people to spread the word about your knitting club? How can you get people excited about being part of your community?

Your compelling positioning and follow-up skills will be

invaluable when it comes to securing venues. How can you show the venue that it would benefit them to let your club use the space? How can you follow up in a non-sleazy way to ensure you get a "yes"?

Or, you can call on your real estate negotiating skills to research, create, and price a highly valuable online course teaching people to knit, or start a virtual knitting group with people from around the world.

You already have a knack for determining value and price point and could easily apply these incredibly advantageous business skills to your side hustle by researching current market offerings that other product/service providers are giving at each price point.

Since your real estate experience taught you the importance of timing, you plan to launch your online knitting course in the months before winter when interest starts to pick up.

Not convinced that knitting sounds like a serious enough side hustle to pursue? I know of a woman who makes six figures teaching knitting online. No talent or experience is too small to profit from. What skills are you downplaying that others might admire and want to learn from?

Once you go through this exercise, you'll see that your skills are more than enough to put you on the path.

When I started as a coach and writer, I didn't have a clue how to pitch editors. But I knew how to build business relationships from scratch, so I started there and learned new skills as I went.

You don't need to know everything right now—you just need to know enough to get started.

Bonus step:
Ask someone you love what you're good at.

We're so used to our own strengths and skills that they don't always stand out to us. But to others, they're clear as day.

If you're struggling with the *Skill Distiller Formula*, try asking a friend or a loved one what you're good at, or what problems you help solve. They'll be able to shine a light onto the strengths you have inside of you. Then take those skills and strategize how they can be useful to you as you build your side hustle.

Once you realize how you can use your strengths to build the business you've always wanted, you'll start to get really excited.

If you're like most people, you'll feel that sense of excitement . . . and then you'll quickly start questioning whether your idea is realistic. Don't! Hold onto your enthusiasm and let the idea grow before trying to poke holes in it!

Some of you might not need this formula. It might be burningly obvious that you have a novel inside you, or that your future is filled with beautiful gardens to landscape or organic baby clothing to design and create. But some of us need a little help. We know what things interest us but can't identify exactly what our passion might be, let alone get started creating a business out of it.

As I've mentioned, Gallup polling from 2013 indicates that only 13 percent of employees worldwide are engaged, or feel psychologically committed, at work, and their 2015 report found that millennials are less likely to say they "have the opportunity to do what they do best" at work, and many are working in jobs that aren't aligned with their talents or strengths. Often, this is because they hold back from pursuing their dreams out of a fear that what they'd really like to pursue, whether it's teaching knitting or something else, isn't viable. The end result? Dissatisfaction.

When I surveyed my blog subscribers, I found alarmingly similar results. Here is what came up:

When asked: **"What scares you the most?"**

+ 43.09 percent of you said: "Not fulfilling my potential here on earth."

+ 28.73 percent said: "Not knowing what I am good at and being stuck in my day job."

When asked: **"How would I feel if my work situation was exactly the same 12 months from now?"**

+ 48.72 percent of you said: "Not good at all."

+ 31.16 percent said: "Okay, I guess."

+ 17 percent said: "Pretty good," and a mere 3.12 percent of you answered: "Happy. I love my job and it's all I want for now."

The comments said it all:

+ "Defeated"

+ "I officially feel stuck and bored"

+ "I'd need antidepressants"

Finally, to the question: **"How much of my current income (as an employee) would I truly be willing to forgo in order to be my own boss?"**

+ 19.50 percent of you said you would give up 30 percent.

+ 23.27 percent said you would give up 20 percent.

+ 28.30 percent said you would give up 10 percent.

+ 28.93 percent were unwilling to sacrifice any of their salary to go out on their own.

I understand that this is somewhat of a loaded question and the way I worded it implies quitting your job altogether. I certainly do not suggest doing this until you have successfully paralleled your hustle with your full-time job and it is completely self-sustaining.

What's important about the responses above are what they say about the status quo. A huge number of people are so unhappy with their work situation they would forgo a large portion of their income to pursue their passion! If that's not an incentive to forge ahead on a side hustle, I don't know what is.

Still scared? Remember this good news: You are not your job. You are much bigger than and not restricted by whatever your job title says you are—even if you love your current career. As I wrote for the health and fitness website Greatist in a piece titled "Your Job Doesn't Define You. Here's How To Discover What Does," the number one reason clients have given for seeking out my life coaching is that they feel limited or unfulfilled by the work they are doing.

They come to me for help figuring out their "purpose" or "calling." All day at work they are humming along, looking happy on the surface, but feeling frustrated. They feel bored. They feel inauthentic, which eats away at their self-esteem. As best-selling author Steven Pressfield puts it, they feel like a "shadow version" of themselves. They know that they have the energy, passion, and smarts to do anything—they just don't know what exactly. Or how to begin.

Sadly, no one is going to hand you your passion (plus instructions to bring it to life!) in an envelope. But there are some important questions you can ask yourself to identify what calls to you and ignites your spirit. Getting quiet, going inward, and being honest about what sparks joy within you—and then taking action to actualize it—is very, very powerful. Listening to your inner wisdom and being guided by it brings with it certain magic.

After you get started with the *Skill Distiller Formula*, you'll need to be clear on what your side hustle might be.

Here are nine questions you can ask yourself:

1. What am I doing when I'm slacking off at work?

My client Dave is a great engineer. When he got an unexpected bonus he spent the entire thing on photography equipment. His weekends are spent taking snapshots of Manhattan and Brooklyn. He follows only photographers on Instagram and reads photography blogs and articles online whenever he is bored in work meetings or has a quiet hour or two to spare in the office. In fact, he spends hours at the office researching photography exhibitions and even planned a trip to a European show. His photography passion was undeniable.

When a friend paid him to take artsy photos for his company website, Dave said to me, "Susie, is this what dying and going to heaven feels like?" Um . . . yes! Disclaimer: I certainly do not suggest you slack off at work, but let's face it, for many of us there is a lot of idle time—and what we spend that idle time doing could be a great indicator for what our side hustle passion is.

2. What brought me joy as a kid?

Believe it or not, your passions may evolve and grow, but they never actually change or leave you. When you were very young, what made you happy—playing music, writing stories, helping animals, being captain of a sports team, building stuff? Jack Canfield, motivational speaker and co-author of the *Chicken Soup for the Soul* series, recommends conducting what he calls a "joy review."

Write down times in your life that you felt most happy. Was it when you backpacked through Asia on a shoestring budget? Led the debate team in high school? Trained junior staff at work? Or decorated your past two apartments? Likely, you'll find a common thread throughout those joyful moments. When you see it all on paper, it's easier to connect the dots.

3. What blogs and books do I love to read?

Think about the top five websites you peruse once you power up your laptop. For example, I worked with a Realtor who spent hours reading recipes in cookbooks, websites, and natural food blogs. He now has a decent following as a food blogger himself and earns a small revenue stream from it. Look at who you follow (aside from friends) on Facebook and Instagram.

4. If money were no object, what would I do all day?

Believe it or not, even rich people need to work to stay stimulated (just look at Oprah Winfrey and Richard Branson). THEY JUST DO WHAT THEY WANT TO DO for that work! Now *that's* freedom. What would you do in this same position? Would you write, teach scuba diving, give dating advice? Work that you would do for free strongly implies what activities you enjoy most and what probably comes pretty easily to you.

5. If I could be anyone for a week, who would it be?

Who we admire is a huge indicator of who we secretly would like to become. Do you look up to Abby Wambach, Sophia Amoruso, Victoria Beckham, Matt Lauer, Erin Burnett? Review who you obsess over—it's a bright, shining clue.

6. What do I feel least insecure about?

Human beings are funny. We are inordinately hard on ourselves, quick to point out our flaws and slow to recognize our skills. I once coached a very high-achieving CEO, and getting her to share her leadership strengths with me was like pulling teeth!

If this sounds like you, instead of thinking which qualities you most value in yourself, ask, "What parts of me do I dislike the least?" Allow yourself to remember past accomplishments or times where you've really helped others. Let the parts of you that you might secretly feel proud of truly shine.

7. What's pure and simple fun for me?

Ain't nothin' like a consistent hobby to reveal an awesome hustle idea. The only difference between a hustle and a hobby is that a hustle pays—meaning it provides a service for others, not just for your own enjoyment. Take note: If you love to paint as a hobby purely for your own pleasure, great! That might not be a hustle idea. But if you'd also love to paint for other people and have your work in other people's homes/offices/beach houses . . . you may just be sitting on a jackpot!

I have one friend who loves Krav Maga and teaches it to families, and another friend who adores planning parties for her entrepreneurial friends. Bingo! They love the work they are doing, they are good at it, and they can be paid for it. What do *you* love to do that you are really good at and can be paid for?

8. What conversation topic never gets boring to me?

What subject brings on that "I could talk about this all day!" feeling? My husband, for example, loves talking about real estate investments—if he had a second job, it would be flipping homes, he always says. It's a total snooze fest for me, but luckily he has a brother and a couple of close friends who share his passion.

It's important to ask yourself not only which topics energize you but which people can get excited about them with you. It's critical to nurture relationships where a common passion unites you. Which leads us to . . .

9. Who is my tribe?

Your tribe consists of people who get you. It might not be your colleagues, your college pals, or even your siblings. A close former coworker of mine found her tribe at a popular local fitness class. When I see her around her tribe, she is the brightest and most energized version of herself. It's awesome!

If you don't have a "tribe" already, you can find one. Use all of the clues above to pinpoint your interest and then locate a group that shares it. Join a book club. Take a cooking class. Learn to code at a local college. Volunteer at an animal shelter. Opportunities and people are everywhere when you open your eyes and look. I found some remarkable tribal pals at New York University, where I spent my Saturdays with people of all ages and professional backgrounds training to become certified life coaches.

Now that you've asked yourself these questions, is a path clearer to you? Great! Once you have some clarity, you have to take action. Nothing, nothing, nothing changes without action. When I started coaching I was working full time as an advertising sales director. I thought I wanted to coach people on how to sell. I enjoyed it, but realized that what I love most is coaching people on how to do something else: harness their personal power to gain confidence and pursue their dreams. I know it's possible, especially after having actualized mine.

Ask yourself: What are three things that I can do over the next seven days to bring my passion to life? Then do them. Set up that YouTube account so you can start posting your instructional videos. Tell your friends and colleagues you're available as a Halloween party planner in exchange for a testimonial. Ask the woman you look up to in marketing if you can buy her a latte for 20 minutes of her time. The options are endless.

The following week, do three more. Then three more. And watch what happens. Keep doing this—never stop doing. The results will astound you once you get busy.

Remember: Anything good that has ever been created has been the result of small, consistent actions. A few dollars here, a few dollars there add up to a sweet sum of savings. Smart lunch choices repeated over time result in a healthier body. This is no accident, and self-exploration is no exception. At any moment you can begin the process of going deeper into yourself and bringing the innermost (gorgeous, ready, willing!) part of you to life.

You are not your job. Your job is one part of your multi-faceted, potential-filled self. And deep down you know it too. What are you waiting for? As the thirteenth-century Persian poet Rumi wrote, "What you seek is seeking you." Your joy, tribe, and bliss are patiently waiting. They will always be waiting. You just need to act.

As a bonus, in some fields, getting your side hustle going on the side can help your star shine brighter in the office! Aaron of NatureMapr works in technology for his day job. His app tracks vulnerable native species using crowdsourcing. After starting his company on the side, he discovered that having made his own product increased his reputation. "[I]t actually gets you a bit of 'street cred' in the technology workplace as well because it's a technology company that you've built by hand and, well, I work in technology. So you're living what you preach rather than just talking about doing something one day."

Don't you want that same type of enhanced reputation as someone who gets things done? So get busy brainstorming!

You just have to pinpoint a passion. Most people have a few, but to start just choose one that fits these criteria: You have a talent for it, people want/need it, and you can make money doing it. It can be anything from teaching calligraphy to planning parties to freelancing as a website creator. Don't overthink it! Your business will change over time, so just begin. What are some of your ideas?

Again, think of someone you know who really believes in you. They can be your spouse, best friend, parent, former manager, anyone at all . . . they don't even have to be in your life (or alive) anymore. It can be a high school teacher or a coach you once had. My dad died when I was 19 and I think of him a lot and what he would say about the work that I am doing now. Think about what this person who believes in you would think about your new business/creative venture. What would they say/tell you?

Now listen: Their faith in you is right. Your doubt is not.

Here are some side hustles that might be right for you to pursue:

+ Flipping houses
+ Proofreading/editing
+ Home fashion consulting
+ Blogging
+ Creating organic skincare products, home cleaning solutions, etc.
+ Event and party planning
+ Producing hampers for picnics

- Teaching English as a second language
- Providing transportation for the elderly or driving with Uber, Lyft, or another "sharing economy" app
- Nutrition/wellness coaching
- Teaching people simplified tax preparation
- Designing logos and other freelance graphic design work
- Nature or wedding photography
- Wedding speech writing
- Catering
- Financial planning for recent college graduates
- Getting certified as a personal trainer or fitness teacher
- E-publishing romantic/steamy short stories
- Options trading
- Creating custom-made bras
- Making organic candles
- Executive business coaching
- Jewelry making
- Selling crafts on Etsy
- Personal shopping or styling
- Running a YouTube channel
- Real estate investing in high-growth markets
- Beekeeping/selling honey
- Making homemade stationery or letterpress
- Refereeing for a recreational or youth sports league
- Social media consulting
- Helping people shoot YouTube videos and offering video editing services

* Providing pet grooming or doggy massages
* Private tutoring
* Freelance grantwriting
* Massage certification
* Doing voice-overs
* Creating and selling knitwear patterns on a platform like Ravelry
* Organizing people's closets
* Teaching yoga or meditation

Over to you ✦ ✦ ✦ ✦ ✦ ✦ ✦ ✦

Brainstorm ten potential hustle ideas. Don't think too much, just write. These can be teaching English as a second language, selling custom crafts on Etsy, peddling your famous cheesecake at the local church—anything. Come up with a *minimum* of ten ideas. You won't feel ready for them all, but that's the point. We want to get our ideas flowing because this will spur our taking action.

Once you have your ten ideas, give each a rating in terms of your enthusiasm, your aptitude, and the idea's feasibility. Share your list with a friend you trust, one who can be an accountability partner and cheerleader (and do the same for them!)

Ask him or her:

* These are my ideas. What do you think?
* What am I most good at here?
* Is there anything I am missing?

Once you have narrowed your list down to one, ask yourself these questions:

- ✦ Who is doing this already? Who are your possible competitors or partners?
- ✦ What platform/format are they using to sell their product or service (for instance, in-person classes, online courses, brick-and-mortar stores, cookbooks, consulting)?
- ✦ What is their pricing structure?
- ✦ How are they marketing/branding their product or service? How are they communicating with their customer/subscriber base, and how frequently (e.g., weekly/monthly emails containing free tips/recipes)?
- ✦ What FREE online resources (or even cheap books) can I use/read to learn more about establishing myself in this niche/industry before spending money on courses or licensing?
- ✦ How can I differentiate my offering and brand?

Answering the above questions will really help address a lot of your initial concerns and give you a sense of the direction you need to be heading. Think about how your own hustle may fit within the framework of these questions.

5

Why a "Vision Board" May Help

"Create the highest, grandest vision possible for your life, because you become what you believe."
—Oprah Winfrey

"The best way to succeed is to have a specific Intent, a clear Vision, a plan of Action, and the ability to maintain Clarity. Those are the Four Pillars of Success. It never fails!"
—Steve Maraboli, best-selling author and motivational speaker

Still struggling with unlocking what your passion might be? A vision board event can help! I have held a lot of these, from small gatherings at my home to corporate and nonprofit events. It's amazing the stories that come from them—one woman thought she wanted a baby, but instead her board was filled with travel images. She wanted to see more of the world first. Another got an idea to create a line of handbags after being drawn to images and locations where she could find materials and create a unique product of her own.

The truth is, many people have trouble pinpointing exactly what it is they want. This makes them feel blocked, stuck, and unclear about their goals. Here are my tips for how to break through that wall by creating a vision board with friends.

Put simply, a vision board is a collage of images and pictures that affirm your dreams and goals (anything that makes you feel happy and inspired), all in one place. Some people call these an inspiration board or a dream board. Vision boards work by helping you get clear on what you want and unlocking the magical flow of manifestation, as through the power of images we can visualize our future for ourselves by putting on paper the visions that "call" to us.

It is a fabulous way to get specific and put your dreams on paper in a unique (and fun) way. A client of mine once put a picture of the Golden Gate Bridge on her vision board and two months later received a job transfer to San Francisco.

Another friend chose an image of a musician playing the piano and then met and fell in love with a man who played in a local band.

In New York City I hold vision board parties for my clients and as part of my workshops. If you want to host your friends at home, this is a wonderfully different way to get together and get a gorgeous result to boot. It's a ticket to open the floor to discuss and share your goals in a supportive environment.

This is all you need to throw a great event at home:

✦ **Open-minded friends**

Vision board parties feed on group energy. Invite your positive, imaginative, and open-minded friends over. Not only will you have a blast, you will create something meaningful together that you can discuss for the entire year (or years) to come. Around six to eight people is a good group size.

✦ **Materials at the ready**

A vision board is something you create from scratch— all you need are some magazines (home, style, fashion, food, business, family), a poster board (from anywhere), scissors, and glue. Tell your friends not to read the magazines. They are a source of inspiration and cutout material only. Your friends can bring their old magazines too (as well as an appetizer or drink if they like!)

✦ **A little bit of scene setting**

Play some soft or uplifting tunes and light a couple of candles. Make it feel a bit more inspired and Zen-like than usual. No television. No phones (unless it's to stream your chill-out playlist). A Zen setting creates an intimate environment that lends itself to a creative and intuitive group mindset.

✦ **Clear instructions and directions**

Not everyone will know how to create a vision board. Explain that it is important not to overthink it. It's simply a matter of creating a collage of images/illustrations and words that "speak" to you. Tear them out of the magazines and arrange them on a page. Tear first, glue later (but everything has to be glued before they leave—no scraps of paper to leave the house).

✦ A visualization or a reading

This is not any old night in. Rather than get carried away with talking and drinking, and forget to focus on your boards, insist that people come over at a certain time, sharp. Then read a short visualization or meditation passage to open the evening to get everyone in the same headspace (there are tons available online if you search for "short visualization/presence/meditation passage"). This will ensure that everyone is focused on the present moment and knows why they are there. You can also do a quick round of introductions (if some of the guests are unacquainted) and everyone can set an intention for their board.

✦ Collaboration and flow

Encourage your friends to talk about their boards and image choices. Creativity begets creativity and group energy can be powerful and magnetic. Also, remember that the theme/ideas can change while in the process of creating the board. You may think you are creating a board for financial success but along the way focus more on home and family life. Enjoy the "aha!" moments and talk about them with each other. This is,

in fact, one of the highlights of vision board creation—
the unexpected desires that surface. Your hustle ideas
will flow freely!

✦ **A little blank space**

Tell your friends to leave a little space on their boards
for anything they see that might inspire them later. They
could even put a radiant, happy picture of themselves in
the center. Explain that it is important to keep the vision
board in a place where they see it every day. This is how
the law of attraction is multiplied.

It's a lot more fun to share this imaginative and artistic
experience with others. And it's a wonderful break from digital distraction that brings people together in a uniting and
unique way. Having partners in crime along the way will
motivate you and spur you on when your energy lags, and you
never know what collaborations may arise.

Over to you ✦ ✦ ✦ ✦ ✦ ✦ ✦ ✦

Set a date. Grab a group of hustlers, or people you know who
just want more from their lives. Then roll up your sleeves and let
the festivities (and manifestation magic) begin. What transpires
might astonish you!

Tweet me what came up for your hustle @susiemoore!

6

Why You'll Never Be "Ready"

"Amateurs sit and wait for inspiration,
the rest of us just get up and go to work."
–Stephen King

"The secret of getting ahead is getting started. The
secret of getting started is breaking your complex
overwhelming tasks into small manageable tasks,
and starting on the first one."   –Mark Twain

You will never, ever, ever be "ready" to start a side hustle. Like many things in life, conditions are never perfect and it never feels like the exact right time to embark on the adventurous journey of launching a business. The sooner you understand this, the better. Getting a dog, moving to a new country, or getting divorced— I have done them all, and I put them all off at different stages of my life. But I needn't have. The result is the same whether you feel prepared for the next step or not. Getting started now just means that you arrive at your destination sooner.

What creeps in here, my friend, with this "being ready" talk is your fear once again. And the only antidote to fear is action. *Immediate* action.

There is a mistake that we make where we *think* we are taking action. Maybe we're doing research, taking a course, going to a million galleries, or reading a thousand books, and we feel we should get the credit for exploring our idea. Not so fast! Consuming relevant materials matters too, of course, but it alone won't result in anything apart from your own increasing knowledge. And the purpose of knowledge is to be used. To inspire. To lead you to create. Knowledge, as Napoleon Hill says in *Think and Grow Rich*, is only "potential power." You've got to **do the work** as well.

I'm very guilty here too. I am a huge reader and could get lost in books for an eternity, but I still had to write this one, not to mention every single blog post and article that comes from my humble little laptop. I have to make my *own* work, not just devour what other writers have created before me. I have to contribute too. That is why we are all here on earth—to make our contribution, however small, and leave the world a little better than how we found it.

I had a client who was passionate about food blogging and could spend four straight hours on Pinterest creating beautiful boards on baking, spring dishes, and party appetizers with table decorations. Fun? Yes. Useful? Maybe. But real work and side-hustlin' this is not. Do not get the two confused. And do not hide behind research or spending thousands of dollars on courses, no matter what they promise. A hustle ain't a hustle until it generates money, so don't get caught in hobby land. Get out of neutral research gear and start moving forward.

Sean Behr of Stratim recommends just diving in. He says, "Get a few customers fast (even free customers). The quickest route is to get your first three customers. You will learn so much from your first three customers and it will save you a ton of time and energy down the road."

Be Careful Investing in the Following:

✦ Flashy Marketing Materials

I see so many people blow money trying to make their business and brand as "beautiful as possible," only to make no money. Promotion does not necessarily mean spending loads of cash on shiny things for your business. You can have a clean, engaging brand with relatively minimal cost. Or at least save your branding expenses for after your initial launch. I am a huge advocate of making money before spending money.

✦ Public Relations

There are so many hack "PR Expert" types out there who will take your money and yield you very little. If you do insist on hiring someone, choose someone with great testimonials who fits within your budget. In my experience, the best PR you can do comes from the relationships you build and the value you offer. Relationship building and reciprocity (helping others before expecting them to help you) is the key!

✦ Expensive Advertising (on- or offline)

Be very careful when it comes to spending money on advertising. More often than not, people throw good money after bad. Don't be trapped into thinking that paying for Facebook likes will lead to loads of business. You want to spend wisely so that any advertising is leading to actual conversions (i.e., somebody going to your site and signing up to your subscriber list). I know, or know of, plenty of people who have big social media followings (much of which was paid for) with tiny email subscriber lists whose businesses make hardly any money. Again, good money after bad.

✦ Course after Course after Course

Courses can be great. I love paying for a good course if it helps me take my business to the next level, and I teach a number of courses myself. But unfortunately, there are many people that are serial course takers, who wait for that spark of inspiration or the "right time" to launch their business and never take any action. *No course will change that.* It's a bit like learning to ride a bike by reading all about it and going to lectures where there are no actual bikes to ride, instead of seeking out a two-wheeler right away. You just have to get on it, baby! Get on, fall off, get back on, and then learn your own technique. To borrow the words of Aristotle, "For the things we have to learn before we can do them, we learn by doing them."

I know getting started is scary. This is what I tell people who panic the moment the time comes to pull the trigger: Get on the bike. It's not about you. You were put on this earth for a greater purpose than the one you are fulfilling—otherwise a side hustle would not ignite your spirit and call to your heart.

Lauren Grant, now the founder of event planning company The Grant Access, had her epiphany moment after getting laid off ten years into a career doing event management for nonprofits. She says, "After getting laid off I realized . . . I can't do this for free anymore. Strangely enough, my epiphany came during a party I was throwing for a friend. It was like the heavens opened up and said, 'You are really good at this!' My network heavily influenced my decision to make The Grant Access official. Having their support, encouragement, and affirmation of my skills gave me the additional push I needed. I had clients before I even had a business name." Like Lauren, you already have everything you need—branding, PR campaigns, advertising, and industry training are just the bells and whistles. Don't let them distract you from the big picture. Sometimes all the pieces are already in place, we just need to see that they're there. We all have a purpose and when we follow what drives our beautiful desires and dreams we are getting closer to it. Your gift, whether you can teach, paint, sell, sing, design, screenwrite, cook, inspire others, train dogs— whatever you have been blessed with the talent for doing—exists to serve the world.

Stop obsessing over whether you are good or worthy enough and just show us what you got! When you give your all to what you love to do and surrender the outcome, you kinda have it all figured out already. With too much focus on the self we lose the meaning and understanding of what life is for: to use our special gifts and talents to make a positive impact on the lives of others.

Remember that your life is part of a much larger whole. It is your job only to figure out what your role is and then to get busy. Don't ask, "What do I want?" but rather, "How best can I contribute?" Let this be the mantra behind your side hustle if you need one. You have something big to contribute and you just know it, don't you? All you have to do is believe in your work, your contribution. You have something great to offer the world! The understanding that it is not about you (and that pesky, fearful ego), it is about your offering, is really very reassuring. We just have to get out of our own way.

If you follow the below tips, you'll get off on your best foot as you shift out of "what if" mode and into action.

✦ Schedule dedicated time

Clear a block of at least four hours a week (in two-hour chunks if you work better in smaller bursts) to get your side hustle action going. Like an appointment or important meeting, this time is neither changeable nor negotiable. Schedule it! Put it in your calendar! Unless someone dies, this is your time to get busy (and not with research—write/create/do). Do not answer the door. Ignore the mess in the kitchen. Your hustlin' time is more important. The beauty is, often these chunks of time grow from two hours to three to four hours without our even knowing the time passes. This is called being in the flow.

✦ Commit to zero excuses

As you get ready to work and whenever you consider your side hustle, guard your mind (more on this to come later). Every time a negative thought creeps in to tell you achieving your goal is not possible, or to hinder you from getting started, release it immediately and consciously. You also might want to limit your time around nonbelievers too, people who are cynical about anything outside of a nine-to-five job. They will say things like, "Come on, it's Sunday, time for a movie/coffee/beer." Success takes sacrifice. You won't regret it later. Remember, only results matter! **Excuses don't.**

✦ Remove distractions

Keep your phone at bay. Shut down all social media and turn off your laptop notifications. Make yourself unavailable for anything or anyone during your hustle time. As I write this, my mail is switched off, as is the messenger on my laptop, which normally pops up anytime there is a text from a friend. Off, off, off. The silence is your friend. To write this book I unsubscribed from almost everything that is in my "self-help/productivity/kick-ass in life" genre. And I follow a lot of people! I was always looking at Instagram seeing what they were up to, what they were promoting, and who with. I had to give myself a self-help book hiatus. As a total junkie of the genre this was hard, but for a couple of months I committed to reading fiction only so I could channel what is inside of me and not be diverted by new ideas or topics. Those tempting books get put on a list for after I wrote THE END, and until then all my mentors and contemporaries were on pause. They might have run for office and I wouldn't even know! You need to be laser-focused to make real progress. Side benefit: This lack of distraction kinda feels good. You may find yourself not even wanting to resubscribe to a lot of online info! What in your own life can you set aside while you pursue your dream?

✦ Set a deadline

We life coaches are ruthless about deadlines. They are crucial for reaching the finish line. What does success look like for you and your hustle? Start with the end in mind and give yourself a clear, achievable, and realistic deadline to make it happen (e.g., by July 31, 12 p.m. EST, I will have finished my novel). Break it up into small, bite-size deadlines, too, to make yourself accountable along the way. Say your novel is twelve chapters. You have six months. So that is two chapters per month. One every two weeks. What are you waiting for? 2029? Remember this too: Until you launch this project there is no room for another project/idea/inspiration to surface. Get this one done by your deadline and get excited about what's next! The next idea will come, I promise.

✦ Enjoy the process!

I know this all sounds very serious. But it's meant to be fun (most of the time, anyway). When we are in the process of doing we are at our most calm, engaged, and creative. Be present and enjoy the flow of your talents as you express them.

For example, I love to write but I hate updating my website and managing the software system that launches my online courses and weekly newsletters. I outsource most of the coding but I still need to have an understanding of it, so in my moments of technological frustration I come back to my "why". Why does it matter? Well, no website? No courses? No infrastructure? No growth. When I first started my business as a hustle it wouldn't have mattered, but removing all of that functionality now would kill the momentum. You take the rough with the smooth— and enjoy the fun parts even more in contrast to the less glamorous but necessary work. As my friend and fellow life coach Stephanie St. Claire says, "Running the business end is the first priority, not consulting or writing. You will spend 15 percent of the time doing what you love (your gift—in my case coaching and writing) and 85 percent of the time marketing, administrating, selling, strategizing your business, and answering a load of email. Survival will totally hinge on how quickly you adopt this role of Business Owner first, creator of pretty things second."

✦ **Celebrate!**

This is my favorite part. You have to celebrate small
wins along the way. When you have had one month
of applied activity towards your goal, treat yourself! A
massage, new motivating book, or glass of champagne
will inspire you to keep going. I love getting a manicure
after a particularly satisfying day of writing—or trying a
new restaurant with my husband. Remember, it's about
the journey, so season that journey with some enjoyable
pit stops.

Over to you ✦ ✦ ✦ ✦ ✦ ✦ ✦ ✦

Feeling inspired? Get started now on the first of your two-
hour blocks! I'll wait.

7

How Do I Find the Time?

"Focus on being productive instead of being busy."
    –Tim Ferriss, author of *The 4-Hour Workweek*

"Once you have mastered time, you will understand how true it is that most people overestimate what they can accomplish in a year—and underestimate what they can achieve in a decade!"
    –Tony Robbins, author & personal development legend

"Insulate yourself from distractions."
    –Jeff Walker, author

"But how do I find the time??" I hear you ask.

It varies depending on the hustle, but you can start your side hustle with just a few hours a week. Fun fact: The movie *Pitch*

Perfect and the novel *Fifty Shades of Grey* were largely written on trains—while Kay Cannon and E. L. James were commuting to work. *Pitch Perfect* grossed more than $65 million in 2012 and *Fifty Shades* $95 million in 2013. (E. L. James topped the Forbes list that year as the #1 highest-earning author.)

Knowing that, do you really need those hours spent playing Candy Crush or stalking people on social media? Do you really need to binge on episodes of *Silicon Valley*? Guess what? None of that will help you retire in Maui!

It's not about time; it's about priorities. We all have 24 hours in a day. To help you make the best of them, I'm sharing with you my ultimate productivity hacks—how to get more done in less time. These are useful whether or not you have a side hustle— they are killer time-saving tips that can help everyone!

✦ Commute wisely

Here is what I do. In the mornings I take a few minutes to consciously write (with intention) in my five-minute journal. If I can help it, I don't check my email or social media until I am out the door. Here is why:

>   2 minutes waiting for elevator
>
>   2- to 3-minute wait for subway
>
>   12-minute subway ride
>
>   3-minute wait for coffee
>
>   1-minute wait for the next elevator

= 21 minutes of social media time to check while idle/waiting, if you must. Use this time to check your Instagram, Facebook and Twitter feed (1–2 minutes each) and then respond to any overnight texts or emails = 15 minutes. Perfect! Also, checking email often causes me stress, and I don't want to think about the needs of other people the first second I wake up. I want to think about my needs, and my journal allows me to do just that.

I enjoy social media as much as the next person and use it to a certain degree in my business. However, a 2015 *Adweek* study showed that users spend an average of 1.72 hours on social media a day! Let's be honest, an hour and 43 minutes a day spent watching stupid videos and comparing our lives to others is a little sad.

✦ Use "wait time" well

As with the above, if I am waiting in line at the grocery store or in Starbucks, waiting for my nails to dry, or waiting for a friend to arrive at brunch, I use those minutes to either catch up on my reading, take some notes for an upcoming product launch, start a blog post/article, shoot my sisters a text to say hi, or respond to some less-urgent emails. Most people have up to one hour of idle wait time on an average day—more if you have an appointment at a hairstylist, doctor, or vet. It adds up! You might just have uncovered the seven or more hours you need to get the day-to-day stuff done, leaving you more time to work on your hustle.

Think about it. Because you have disputed and corrected that phone/medical bill via a phone call while walking to the supermarket (I like to call AT&T while walking/doing—there is so much on-hold time) and responded to that business contact while waiting in line, you now have 30 free minutes to spend in your evening to do some real work on your business. Do the stuff on the fly that can be done on the fly. Conserve your hours using these little pockets of wait or commute time to give you freedom and clear your head to do your real work at home.

◆ Say no, then say it again

"No" is one of my favorite words. You wanna know why it's so magical? Because when you say no to what doesn't serve you, you say YES to yourself (and the things that serve you). Mastering the art of saying no has been life changing for me. I call "No" the new black. Time is a completely nonrenewable resource, and when used and planned correctly, it's our friend, not our enemy. (How often do we hear people say, "I don't have time?" That is enemy-talk.)

When there are many things going on, breathe, take a moment, and let your intuition decide what makes most sense. A run or brunch? Drinks with a friend or two hours spent on your blog? Before accepting an invitation, think, "Am I genuinely excited or looking forward to this?" If yes, go for it! If you're not certain, say you will let the person know. If not, politely decline. A simple "Thank you so much for the invite, so sorry I can't make it" will suffice. Do it. It gets easier with time, I promise. We all have 24 hours in a day—including Beyoncé—you know the best ways to spend yours.

If you say no to one social dinner/drinks a week plus one meeting a week—including commute time each way—what is that, eight or nine hours? That is the equivalent of a whole workday on your hustle! Don't attend things purely out of the fear of missing out (FOMO). Respect your schedule and people will respect you for it.

Another option is to catch up with friends all at once. When my side hustle really started to grow, I was not only working a very busy job but I was traveling a lot for work too. I felt like I was constantly letting people down by turning down plans and not being very active on the social scene. So I held some parties! This allows a lot of people to come together at once. Inviting a group of people into your home also allows you to connect with others, a key to building awesome, lasting relationships. Reserve a Friday or Saturday night, and tell your friends to come over and bring a bottle. Serve some simple appetizers, play some cool tunes, and boom! You've caught up with everyone, and everyone gets to meet new people. There is nothing as lovely and intimate as a house party. The few hours spent in prep and tidying are a good investment.

✦ Run errands on work time (if you can)

This is a bit of a controversial one and I recommend using discretion, but I see a lot of people do this really successfully. No one (well, no one I have ever met) is busy every minute of the workday. They might say they are or look like they are, but there are a lot of wasted minutes in every day, I can assure you. Think about Friday afternoons at 4 p.m. or an idle Wednesday when the office is quiet and your to-do list is done. Don't resort to Facebook or Instagram or your favorite shopping site. Do some easy, quick errands, which frees up hustle time later.

Here are some things you can do on your downtime at work:

Pay any non-automated bills online.

Buy home essentials on Amazon.

Book your dog or cat in for the vet.

Visit doctor/dentist (they're hard to book after hours).

Go to the post office.

Go to the bank.

Plan what to cook that evening.

Make appointments with hairdresser, accountant, etc.

Some people go to the gym or take a spin class during their lunch hour. Great idea! Then from 5 or 6 p.m., depending on your profession, the evening is yours. Doing all of this, when possible, on work time can save hundreds of hours over time for side hustle action after work and on the weekends.

✦ Make phone calls on the go

Who do you need to call? Do it while moving! I catch up with friends on the phone while walking to and from the subway, unloading my dishwasher, buying stuff at Walgreens, or walking my dog. I carry my headset everywhere so I can make calls or listen to podcasts. Side note: Listen to inspirational podcasts that keep you focused and motivated—you'll find my favorites at the back of this book.

✦ Unsubscribe

If you are anything like me, you get a lot of junk email from airlines, beauty/retail sites, news sites, and more. Do yourself a favor and lose 90 percent of it. Unless you live to hear from that person or company, just clean out your inbox. Fewer distractions that clutter your inbox really help free up space in your brain as well. When it comes to important emails that can't be avoided, it can be more efficient to pick up the phone and respond to people verbally than reply and create a back-and-forth chain. When we're in a rush, our haste can come across in email in an alienating blunt tone—a phone call avoids this.

✦ Drop something

In 2014, I heard Arianna Huffington speak at her *Thrive* conference in New York. She said something that astounded many in the audience: "One of the best ways to complete a project is to drop it." Ha! What a brilliant idea. She said some projects on her to-do list were things like learn to ski and learn German. But she decided to just drop them altogether. Just like that! What an awesome idea (and relief).

✦ Forgive yourself

It's OK to give yourself permission to miss something every so often—a workout, book club, whatever is regularly scheduled in your calendar. Success does take some sacrifice, so give yourself a little break. You will be there next time!

✦ Watch television when doing the mindless stuff

I admit it might be impossible to completely give up my favorite shows, so I recommend using TV time to do stuff that needs to get done but requires very little brainpower. For example, I respond to people that I cannot help and refer them to people who can while I am watching Bravo. And, I'll say it again, don't binge-watch!

✦ Outsource

Outsourcing has been a huge time saver for me. I outsource tasks ranging from researching someone I am about to interview to website updates to basic bookkeeping. Outsourcing allows you to delegate tasks that are an inefficient use of your time—and often at a very reasonable price. My go-to for finding help is the freelance marketplace Fiverr—look for more info in the appendix on other great resources!

✦ Get to know your flow

On my best days, I book nothing before noon apart from writing time. I try to not even open any email accounts if I can avoid it. If something urgent happens I will get a phone call. The morning is when I'm like a supercharged version of myself. I can write 2,000–3,000 words on a good morning. I could never do this after 4 p.m., when I'm an uncreative robot.

Figure out your rhythm—when you are the best version of yourself. If you are like me, use your mornings. Some people rock out at night. Use your best brain for your most important work. When I still had my full-time job, I would get up early and pitch five ideas to my editors before 6:30 a.m. I would write a blog post (or half a blog post). I would set up important side hustle meetings. Then I would move on to the rest of my day knowing I had already accomplished something great. Use your most productive hours for your hustle. There is no way I would let a workout, a non-urgent email from my boss, or a sink full of dirty wine glasses get in the way of my most important producing time.

Research indicates that we have a maximum of three to four "good" hours in the day to produce, to be energized, to be at the top of our game. These are called our golden hours. Dan Ariely, founder of The Center for Advanced Hindsight, believes our golden hours are the first two hours after waking, but you have to do what works for you. You might be a night owl—don't be shamed for that! The only shame we should feel is when an important task takes three-and-a-half hours when it could have taken one hour if we just applied ourselves to completing it in our golden time. I am writing this very sentence at 7:47 a.m. If I had to write it at 3:47 p.m. it would be a *much* slower process.

Scheduling our day to maximize these hours for our hustle makes all the difference. There are other moments that pop up in life too, like a Sunday at 5 p.m. when you find yourself a little bored or restless and unable to concentrate. Before you succumb to Facebook or scrolling your contacts for someone to call, think, "What do I feel I never have time to do that I could use this time for?" I like to use it to write thank-you cards or clean out my bathroom drawers. Getting this stuff done not only feels good but frees space for more hustle time in the following days.

Stephen Covey, author of the best-selling book *The 7 Habits of Highly Effective People*, says something I live by and quote often: "Don't prioritize your schedule, schedule your priorities."

Here are some other top hacks I've learned from fellow entrepreneur friends:

- When on the phone, walk around, tidy up, empty the fridge, fold your laundry.
- Turn off all social media notifications on your phone and laptop.

◆ Plan the next day's outfit on your commute home.

◆ When waiting for someone (in person or on the phone), write a to-do list or respond to old emails and texts.

◆ Do squats while drying your hair/brushing your teeth.

◆ Go with a friend to get a manicure or go for a walk, doubling up your pampering and fitness to-dos with friendship catch-ups.

◆ Catch up on motivational podcasts while running errands such as dry cleaning or going to the bank, to the pharmacy, or out on a jog!

◆ Skype loved ones while you are cooking.

◆ Obey the two-minute rule: if you can do it in two minutes, do it on the spot! This prevents a mammoth to-do list buildup.

◆ Every Sunday night, spend four minutes planning the week ahead.

And yes, you will feel tired sometimes. That's OK! Power through it by focusing on your end goal. My friend Lauren Grant, owner of her own party planning company, The Grant Access, says, "Finding the energy to side hustle is the hardest part! It's literally a second full-time job at times, so juggling my side hustle and my full-time work can be challenging. Some nights I'm just not up to another two to three hours of work, but I push through it because I KNOW I'm walking in my purpose."

And what is more important than that?

Over to you ✦ ✦ ✦ ✦ ✦ ✦ ✦ ✦ ✦

Look at your calendar for next week and find three things you can skip—a social event you don't really want to go to, a workout class you can live without, an errand you can do quickly during work time. Cancel cancel cancel! You've just found yourself some extra hustle time.

8

Think Big but Start Small

*"Adversities, no matter what they are, simply don't hit us
as hard as we think they will. Our fear of consequences
is always worse than the consequences themselves."*
    –Shawn Achor, founder of GoodThink

*"There are always plenty of reasons not to do some-
thing, to give up, go back to the desk job. Approaching issues from the destructive perspective will
guarantee that you fail. You're a hell of a lot
better at making things happen than you realize!"*
    –Mary Keane-Dawson,
    founder of How She Made It

This chapter is for all of you who struggle to assert boundaries that
honor your own needs over those of work, family, friends, or the
world at large. Here's an email exchange from my days as an employee:

Subject: Today

Good morning. Sorry but I need to take a personal day today. I have a 2:30 p.m. meeting, which I have just rescheduled for Thursday. I also have email access and will be aware if anything happens with X client. If you need anything urgent, please call my cell.

See you tomorrow.

Warmly,
Susie

Response: "No worries. See you tomorrow, Susie!"

Well, well, well. Look what happens when you take a day off work. Nothing. Surprisingly for me that day, no one died. Funnily enough, it also did not make the 6 p.m. news. Matt Lauer didn't call me for an interview and the guy from *Dateline* didn't show up on my doorstep with his camera crew.

Let's get real for a minute here. Say you wanted to take one or two days off work to do some research on your side hustle, bang out some meetings (with the bank, a blogger you want to meet, the designer who is working on your logo), or finally complete your book; Cheryl Strayed went to the woods for three weeks to complete her best-selling book, *Wild*, even though she had small children, as just one example. Sometimes, you just need to squeeze in some time off. I took a vacation day when I interviewed Kris

Jenner, for example. I did not want to risk an urgent mandatory meeting from my boss to interrupt our call, or a last-minute client request to ruin a meeting that took me ages to schedule.

Guess what? You can do it too! No one else's life is going to drastically change because you press "pause" on your other obligations. So many people think: Time off? No way! Not me, I can't. Their involvement seems too crucial to step away even briefly. But even the president of the United States takes time off. Sometimes when we fear something it seems more serious than it is. What we think *might* happen is often so far removed from reality.

A couple of years ago I met someone who was proud of the fact that he never takes time off work. I spoke about a holiday I was planning. "I could never take that much time off," he said. He worked at LinkedIn. I asked him why not. He did not seem to have a specific reason, he just told me that he was "working on some important projects." I wanted to tell him that I was sure some time off would help him relax and refuel and that his colleagues would probably cover his work responsibilities while he was away. Plus, "important projects" never stop coming.

I understand that in some cases taking a day or two off can be difficult. But it is very likely that your employer will forget that time off in a week or two's time—and it could have a lifelong impact on your own personal business. Sometimes we need a bit of perspective to help us move forward.

What can this one fear of taking time off work teach us about how we catastrophize so much in our lives? Our brains can automatically assume the worst, when actually the reality is far different—and that goes doubly for our fears around starting a new venture.

So you start your side hustle and it takes longer to get off the ground than you hoped . . . So what? Maybe some setup costs are a little more than you hoped. So what? You are learning! You want to invest $0 or very little to start. Hugely successful lifestyle website mindbodygreen was started with very little investment. Jason Wachob told me:

> "I'm a huge believer in bootstrapping and not raising capital until you are 100 percent certain you know how and are ready to scale. Bootstrapping forces you to focus on building a brand and a great product and finding creative ways to grow revenue—the essentials of a strong business. You need to learn how to grow without throwing money at growth. You'd be surprised how far you can go with so little capital. We started mindbodygreen with nothing. (I think Tim, Carver, and I pooled together $5K in 2007.) The only essential you need to start a business is passion. You can always find capital, you can always find a market, but if you don't have passion then you're in trouble."

Say you don't have a ton of traffic to your new, beautiful website in your first week (you won't). Say the editor at *Esquire* or *Cosmopolitan* rejects your submission. (I have been rejected well over 200 times.) SO WHAT? Patience pays. My friend Rupa says of looking back and starting her business, "I saw a sign the other day (while stuck in traffic, no less) that said, 'Relax. You'll get there when you get there.' Advice and mentors are of course huge assets along the way, but I wouldn't have done anything differently, and I think 'younger Rupa' should just enjoy the ride!"

How can *you* let go of fear and enjoy the ride? "So what?" is one of my favorite questions that I ask myself for perspective. I'm a very impatient person. It's a mixed virtue. I was always in a hurry to succeed and wanted a booming business yesterday. But success takes time. Get to know this now. That is why the side hustle is so killer—it builds over time while you are working at your day job until it's ready for your full-time commitment.

We all experience defeat and setbacks. It's part of life and definitely part of business. My first online product launch sold only two units. A friend of mine held her first music event at a venue in New York that could have hosted 60 people and 11 came (two were her parents). Many authors only reach some level of success after releasing their third, eighth, eleventh book.

As they say, the journey *is* the way. It takes that product launch, that first party, those few books to show you what you need to do. How to get better. What to do next. You can't go places without taking these first steps. In fact, a big-time CEO I know told me he has been bankrupt twice. TWICE! Now he is flying high again in the business world. He also said he would have had to declare bankruptcy a third time if a single client did not come through with payment one morning, as he wouldn't have been able to make payroll. I'm not saying you need to write 11 books or go bankrupt, but I am saying setbacks happen. They are not the end of the road. They light the path for your next steps.

And when you keep going after encountering an obstacle, people will notice. Mary Keane-Dawson, managing director at media agency Neo@Ogilvy and founder of the How She Made It initiative, agrees: "It sounds glib but you have to learn that people respect you because you TRY, even if you don't make it work the first, second, or even third time. People who try are always in demand, and opportunity, in my experience, is more likely to seek out a trier over a thinker any day of the week."

Recently, I started reading the best-selling novel *A Little Life*, which was short-listed for the Booker Prize. Author Hanya Yanagihara wrote it over 18 months while working full time as deputy editor of *T: The New York Times Style Magazine*. This was no mean feat or accident on her part. It took work! It's amazing what can happen when you apply yourself. If you're still feeling stuck, it may be that more than cutting out extra social commitments is needed.

Thomas Edison said, "If we did all the things we are capable of, we would literally astound ourselves." What would happen if you applied an hour a day to your side hustle? Two hours? Five days a week? What is the best that can happen? Look at Hanya. I don't think she was getting wasted at too many bottomless brunches while she worked on her manuscript. Heck, your side hustle can even save you money when you think about the socializing it prevents you from doing. You are making money rather than spending it. Not only that, you're investing in yourself and your future.

Remember this: It's a side hustle! While you build your new business you will still be busy with a job that pays the bills. But this is not an excuse to go slow or to put it off. As my friend Mary says, "I have not followed a career plan but more of an objective/ goal-driven strategy. Every time I reached my goal, and often when I have been traveling between goals, I have had an eye on the next peak I want to climb."

I follow a similar approach by setting six-month goals for myself. I consider these the perfect-size spurt to get things moving in the present moment for a not-too-distant achievement.

There is an old Chinese proverb that I love: "The best time to plant a tree was 20 years ago. The second-best time is today." The future is created in the present moment. Let go of your fear, and leap. Do it now, do it now, do it now.

Over to you ✦ ✦ ✦ ✦ ✦ ✦ ✦ ✦

What can you do today, *right now* (however small) that will benefit your side hustle and shake off your catastrophizing? Make it happen.

Create a list of your side hustle to-dos. Rank them in order of priority. It should take shape naturally and each task will give way to the next to unfold. Keep your to-dos to six to avoid feeling overwhelmed. And start each point with a verb! For example:

"Call Tony re his website advice."
"Craft and practice my new elevator pitch."
"Email editor at *Shape* magazine."

Not just:

"Tony"

"Elevator Pitch"

"*Shape*"

Let the action words inspire your action and get you going!

9

A Killer Way to Sell without Being a Sleaze

"If you would take, you must first give."
–Lao Tzu

Remember, unless you're making sales, your side hustle is a hobby and nothing more. It won't have the power to change your life unless it's creating income for you. You can blog and post on Instagram and give friends favors until the cows come home, but until the payment hits your account or your PayPal gets pinged, you are in hobby land, my friend, and you are not reading a hobby book. We want the money, honey.

Sales can be seen as a dirty word, but there is no business without cash flow. If you take anything away from this section let it be to position your product or service as valuable to your customers. Additionally, before you ask for anything, you need to be a giver of value. A great way to do this is to write. Believe me, you don't have to be a perfect writer—or even a great writer.

But writing can grow your business more quickly than almost anything else. Sharing your ideas and tips and information is a wonderful, free way to get people to know about you. You can do this in a blog, on Twitter, or even by pitching articles to online publications or to more prominent bloggers, who often trade guest posts.

I wrote a lot for free and built a small audience before I asked to get paid as a coach or writer. The incredibly wise thinker Gerd Leonhard taught me many years ago that attention is the most important currency. He said, "Don't ask who pays but who pays attention." Writing is an incredible way of checking the pulse on exactly who is paying attention to exactly what. Based on the views, shares, and comments on your work, you know what is touching people. What they want to know more about. Where there is hunger, interest, a market. The Internet is totally transparent. And that is awesome.

To show you how simple it is, here is an example of a pitch email I wrote to an editor—I keep it simple. Feel free to use it!

Hope you are well, Jenny!

I am a writer for The Huffington Post and mindbodygreen (as well as others).

My author pages are here:

http://www.huffingtonpost.com/susie-moore/
http://www.mindbodygreen.com/wc/susie-moore

I am working on an article regarding 10 Reasons Why Courthouse Weddings Are Kick-Ass—The Best Modern Option. I am sharing my wedding experience at City Hall in New York—why it was one of the greatest decisions of my life and the best way to start our marriage in our twenties.

Not only are these ceremonies easy, inexpensive, and romantic (as it is just you and your beloved)—a surprising amount of celebrities do it: Matt Damon, Jessica Alba, Keira Knightley, even Marilyn Monroe and Joe DiMaggio.

Weddings are a great source of stress, family strain, and debt. Courthouse weddings negate all this. You are just as married with a lot less worry, more time to plan a honeymoon (and where to live), plus money in the bank to enjoy for more lasting things! I believe your audience would find great value in this piece.

I hope you find this story compelling and I look forward to hearing from you, Jenny!

Many thanks
Susie

There are three things that I often repeat when pitching a story (or anything else, for that matter):

1. **Keep it personal.** People love to connect on a human level and we all love stories. Human beings are wired to absorb and soak in stories. Have you noticed how all great speakers often start with a story? Use your own.

2. **I speak about bringing value to an audience.** I talk about being "in my twenties" and that the audience, most likely on a budget, can get "great value" from my tips. For this editor and her team, who need fresh, daily posts, I am offering interesting and relevant content. I did not say how it was my lifelong dream to be published by this great magazine (although it has been one of my goals for a long time), or anything about what was in it for me.

3. **Stay current.** This particular article was published the week Kim and Kanye got married—in a courthouse. You are likely to get a higher success rate when you pitch ideas that are relevant and topical!

The real success comes in the follow-up. I followed up with this editor seven-plus times, along with many others who never responded. This means that in order to get published once, I sent around 50 emails. In the end the partnership I created with this publication resulted in twenty-plus paid articles in just a few months and gave me access to interview an array of celebrities. It also gave me leverage to write for more publications. Start small. Dream big. Don't take no for an answer. That goes for you even if pitching articles isn't your chosen venue. Maybe you're pitching possible new clients or trying to secure a partnership with a venue to host your fledgling event. Either way, persistence and optimism in the face of rejection are key. And even if writing isn't your main goal, don't overlook it as a way to elevate your profile.

In fact, Sara Blakely of Spanx fame says that "no means nothing." She told me that people ripped up her business card in her face. Interviewing her was not only a pleasure, it was also an eye-opening exercise. We often think successful people had it easier than us until we learn how much failure and adversity they endured. They just kept going anyway—giving up is the only guarantee you won't succeed that there is. My own experience has proved that people and opportunities are way more reachable than you think, once you cast the net wide and remain consistent. Getting paid by a large and prestigious publishing house also massively boosted my confidence. I felt like a real writer—hell, I *was* a real writer! And it became increasingly clear that there are way fewer limits than we think there are—no matter how many writer/artist/freelance friends you have who say there is "no work out there." This doesn't apply just to pitching articles, either—whatever your chosen passion and side hustle field is, you can find a niche in it if you're persistent and optimistic.

You have to position yourself as a professional.

There is a huge advantage for people who know how to talk about, package, and position their offering (whatever it may be) and ask for what they want—a job, an introduction, a new client, an opportunity. The people who get hired, get the gig, land the deal are schooled in something beyond mere credentials: simple asking savvy. Sure, they are huge providers of value (they have to be to sustain any kind of longevity), but you can be the best life coach/yoga teacher/investment adviser in the world and it doesn't mean anything if no one knows about you. To me there is nothing more painful, sadder, or more maddening than unused, dormant talent. It makes me want to scream! We are all occasionally guilty of letting our talents lie sleeping, but some of us commit this crime much more than others. We know who we are, and often it's out of a reluctance to promote ourselves.

To make sure this doesn't apply to you, follow the advice of Turn Left founder Fiona McKinnon—the woman who has been my mentor for many years. "Be prepared to put yourself out there. These days that doesn't just have to be in the real world but it can be through online and social relationships as well. Every conversation, and I mean *every* conversation, can create business for you, whether it be an idea, a contact, or an invaluable second opinion, all the way through to a contract or sale."

Networking without research is only a half job, however, so keep on top of trends, your competitors (who can also be partners), and general economic and market influences that can generate lead ideas or a shift in positioning. And follow up! I keep a list of people to speak to each week with no agenda other than to keep relationships strong. If you build genuine, strong relationships I believe that when the time is right, the opportunities will arise. My first year of business was driven by a mixture of friends of friends (old and new), Facebook, LinkedIn, contacts through charity work, and free business network events. Finally, please, say thank you when someone does take the time out of their day to listen, offer advice, give you their business card, or talk about your hustle. However small you may feel the gesture was at the time, it meant something to them as well—and you never know where chance meetings might lead.

Here are some techniques and tricks I learned throughout my ten years in sales that I apply to many areas of my life:

✦ **You gotta own what you have to offer**
Be clear, specific, and assertive about what you are good at. Focusing on your strengths will get you much further, much faster than worrying about your weaker areas.

✦ **You have to explain it in a way that people understand**
Don't overcomplicate. Even the best doctors and scientists explain things in simple ways, for people of any age to interpret. Can you explain your hustle in just a sentence? You will lose your target market's attention if your message/offering is too complex.

✦ **Give, a lot, before asking**
This afternoon, I'm going to a yoga class that offers the first two weeks unlimited for $25. (If I went every day that would be only $3.50 per class.) Airbnb hosts often start their listing at a lower rate while they build credibility. If you go to European Wax Center, your

very first service is 50 percent off. Smart companies give before they ask. In online publications this is pretty much the law of getting started. In order to be paid to write you need to write a lot for free first, show some samples of your work, and ideally have a following (even if very small.) A personal blog completely counts! Most people slip up here. I hear them say things like, "Why would I put free instructional videos on YouTube? People should pay for those!" or "Why would I do a guest blog post on that person's blog? I don't want to give their blog any of my good material." This is completely the wrong approach.

✦ Invest in other people

Give your time, energy, and in some cases, a little money. My biggest hobby is to read. I read a lot and therefore make a lot of recommendations. I have a trick that has worked really well for me for years. If I meet someone I love, or want to thank someone for their advice, or simply feel called to give something (this happens often to me—remember, it's all about the giving!) I send them a book. It can be a digital book or a physical book—both are great. You can gift a Kindle book via Amazon immediately if the recipient has a Kindle. People are so touched by books, especially ones that are useful to them. Try quantifying the price of a touching, helpful book—you can't! The returns are endless. Some are even less than $5. Plus—no one gives

anyone anything for free, so it's extra special. Try it!
Also, be a connector. This is important. Connect people
with opportunities and with other people.

✦ Be open!—To help, and to your own gut

Fiona McKinnon says it best: "Do your research, join
online groups, don't underestimate the benefits of
professional help. I have an accountant, financial adviser,
and coach/mentor that have all been instrumental in
keeping me on track. But, it has to come from you, so
really consider what your side hustle means to you.
Then, every day do something to achieve that goal. I
carry a notebook with me and I am constantly writing
down strategies, ideas, contacts, names, products, plans.
The aha moment for the startup Turn Left came to me
on a bus in India! My second project has been with me
since I was 14 years old, but the time to bring it to life is
right now." Keep yourself ready for inspiration whenever
it may strike.

Over to you ✦ ✦ ✦ ✦ ✦ ✦ ✦ ✦

Think about where the people who might want to buy your
product or service can be located online and offline. What do
they read? Where do they hang? Brainstorm websites that you
can pitch ideas to and see what their articles are about. If you are a
health coach maybe you could pitch to *Shape* magazine an article
called "Five things you don't know about kale." If you are a career

counselor maybe you could post on LinkedIn about "ten common résumé mistakes." This is called "content marketing," and it can work for any type of business. Where are your potential clients and what can you teach them in 500–800 words?

10

The Why and the How of Self-Promotion

"You wouldn't worry so much about what others think of you if you realized how seldom they do."
–Eleanor Roosevelt

"If being an egomaniac means I believe in what I do and in my art or music, then in that respect you can call me that . . . I believe in what I do, and I'll say it."
–John Lennon

Here's the cold, hard truth. It's no one else's job to promote you but *you*. How would you feel if your burning desire that wants to manifest as a killer side hustle remains silent out of a reluctance to put your idea forward? If you, in the words of Wayne Dyer, "die with your music still inside you," are you OK with that? I doubt that very much. Besides, other people are too concerned with their own stuff—their bills, their weight, their Facebook account—to judge your new entrepreneurial venture. So put it out there!

I was terrified when I put out my first video. These were the thoughts circling in my mind:

+ *"WTF? Everyone is going to think I am so dumb/ showy/full of myself!"*

+ *"Who actually cares about what I have to say?"*

+ *"Oh man, my frenemies are just gonna laugh their heads off."*

+ *"I look gross. It's too close up. I should have thought this through more."*

+ *"Once I post this it's for life. It's not safe."*

Now I put out videos regularly and feel a twinge of both nerves and excitement when a new one comes out. The philosopher Goethe said, "Everything is hard before it is easy." Of course I hope people like my videos. But the process is no longer terrifying like it used to be and I can survive if some people don't like them.

One of the most common concerns people have when I coach them is putting the work they are doing "out there." I totally get it. The fear of getting started is one hurdle to overcome, but it's not the last. The fear of putting out your work and letting people see what you're doing is another biggie. When I was working full time I had this nagging feeling that I was waiting for my "real life" to begin. It, of course, already had. I had found my real life's work but was just so scared to talk about it.

I started by telling my friends one by one about how I was training as a life coach, sharing with them the course that I was taking. Share your own steps with those close to you. Your friends will congratulate and support you. (If they don't, find new ones!) But my friends were not necessarily going to be my clients. I had to generate some. And there are no clients without awareness. You've got to put the word out about your work and promote yourself. You can be the best life coach/interior designer/ stand-up comedian on the planet but it doesn't mean anything unless other people know about it.

I started a newsletter that I sent out on Sundays—and still do—to my entire contact list (with permission to unsubscribe, of course). I shared some of my favorite quotes, insights that I had on various life topics, and snippets/stories from the great books I was reading by Deepak Chopra, Jack Canfield, James Altucher, Tim Ferriss, and Marianne Williamson. I've listed them at the back of this book, too, since their inspirational power is an incredible motivating force.

I grew this mailing list by emailing every single contact in my LinkedIn, Facebook, and Twitter networks, asking if they would like to be added to my free weekly wellness newsletter. I had more than 3,000 contacts on LinkedIn alone that I had grown over my career in sales at the time, and as a result my list grew to around 700 people within weeks. I also shared some of my own work on LinkedIn. This was a really subtle way of letting people know about the work I was doing—and by reading my content they got to know my coaching style.

I wanted to personalize each message I sent so that my offering came across as less spammy and more authentic. After all, I did have a personal relationship with most of these people. At the time, LinkedIn wouldn't allow me to do the mail merge kind of message I was looking for, incorporating each person's first name and bulk emailing, so I hired a virtual assistant from Brickwork India to send out approximately 3,000 individual messages through my profile! It probably cost me a few hundred dollars and it took my assistant around 25 hours. The cost was well worth it, as I could focus my attention on being paid to coach and it got things moving with my subscriber list. This turned out to be a great productivity hack. Lesson learned: Don't try and be a hero by taking on absolutely every task in your business. Analyze the opportunity cost. What are you really giving up by trying to "save money" taking on a task yourself? Time? Even more money?

Then, in every third newsletter or so I would share that I had coaching slots open and this drove a lot of referrals my way. I also changed my Twitter account and Facebook profile over time to reflect my life-coaching work rather than my corporate job.

If you read the above and think "I can do that too!" great, get started! But if your reaction was horror at reaching out to so many distant acquaintances, it's time to get over it. You may be proud to be a quiet achiever, but making peace with self-promotion matters.

Before you recoil, let me share a little secret. Shyness, being reserved, being cool, or whatever we default to as our reason for not self-promoting does not necessarily equal humility. We don't wish to put ourselves on the line for criticism so we do nothing and mask it with an overly modest "Oh, I'm not a self-promoter."

Let me share with you why there is nothing brave or beneficial about that. If I learned anything from my decade-long corporate sales career, it's that we are ALL in fact selling something, all the time. Every single one of us. Promotion is not reserved for smooth-talking Realtors or those rocking retail careers. Teachers, HR professionals, and dog walkers are all unofficial salespeople too. We all persuade and influence other people every day. In our résumés, in our self-evaluation performance reviews at our job, in the way we dress, with our very selectively chosen, super-considered social media posts, on our Tinder profiles, *everything*—we are all selling who we are and what we offer the world, constantly.

So why should we be afraid to promote something, a side hustle/business, that exists to impact the lives of others? We shouldn't!

Get used to the fact that it's the new normal. Do you flinch when you see someone sharing a recent job promotion online or an exciting development in their business? I doubt it. We expect to see these posts and when we like the person (and we almost always do if we are following them), we cheer them on. Other people will do the same for you. And if they don't? Well, that's cool too. Leave them to it. I spent an hour talking to Kris Jenner when I interviewed her. She said to me: "It's sad that there are people somewhere, hiding behind their computer and writing cruel things about others on social networks. As my life has evolved and I have been on my own journey, I certainly feel vulnerable and beaten down at times but I know the importance of brushing myself off and getting back up." Whatever you think of her, she has created a billion-dollar family empire. Criticism can't change that!

Let's say, however, that the world of Kardashian-style self-promotion strikes horror in your heart. Surely you have friends or acquaintances who are immersed in the social-media world and feel at home with self-promotion. Ask them to help you!

Derek Flanzraich, the founder of Greatist, says that "In the early days people told me over and over again that I shouldn't be ashamed or embarrassed to ask for help—but I was. I considered it a weakness. As I continue my journey I realize how powerful asking for help can be, because I always needed a lot of help, but I felt like my job was not to ask for it; to pretend I knew the answers. The real truth is I know less of the answers than I ever thought, but in asking for help, you unlock the opportunity to receive help."

You may not know the first thing about how to create publicity, but a friend might be able to guide you through it—if you ask! Your side hustle will always be your responsibility, but getting advice on how to spread the word about it might be just what you need to let you focus on improving the value of what you are offering.

Self-promotion means you will only want to put your best work out into the world, as you are accountable for it. It opens up opportunities too. When an online startup is looking for a consultant to lead a project, or newlyweds are seeking out an interior designer, who will be on the top of their mind? The people they hear about who are doing great things! Don't let self-consciousness prevent you from progressing.

And as for what people think? James Altucher talks about the rule of thirds. One-third of people will like you, one third of people won't like you, and the other third won't care about you. Focus on the third that counts!

Create an Elevator Pitch

It will also help if you get comfortable speaking about your project. That's where an elevator pitch is invaluable. Every side hustler needs one! Now, what is an elevator pitch, exactly? It's a way to simply and easily describe your product or service in a snap. More than anything, it needs to be clear and concise to draw people in.

In order to have a good elevator pitch you need a few key components to get your message across. This template will help you do just that.

First, the elevator pitch should answer the question, "Who are you?" This is your answer if I were to meet you at an event or casually at a friend's brunch and ask, "What do you do?" It shouldn't just be your name—it should be an enthusiastic description of your unique skills!

Don't be shy about the last part: proclaiming what makes you the best! It's important to stand out if you want to attract business.

In order to get this rolling, all you have to do is get clear on your product or service that's for sale, who you serve, and why it's YOU that's delivering it.

So don't just give your name or role. Be specific and answer all of the following questions in your introduction:

+ My name is . . .
+ I am a . . .
+ I specialize in . . .
+ What I do is . . .
+ What makes me the best is . . .

Then, end with a request or call to action . . . e.g., *Could this be useful to someone you know? Here's how to reach me.*

Here are some examples:

My name is Katy.

I am a photographer.

I specialize in maternity photos.

What I do is help women feel their most gorgeous, natural, and comfortable in their beautiful final stages of pregnancy.

What makes me the best is how I help women feel at ease so that their true essence comes through on camera and shows in the results.

Could this be useful to someone you know?

I take new client consultations Tuesdays and Thursdays after 6 p.m.

My name is Jonathan.

I am a social media expert.

I specialize in Instagram for business.

What I do is help people use the most engaging social media channel to attract new clients who would never have discovered them otherwise.

What makes me the best is that I worked at Facebook and know the insider algorithmic secrets. I also grew my own following to 30K in six months.

Do you know anyone who could be interested in growing their business? I take new client consultations on Saturday afternoons.

My name is Amy.

I am a beauty blogger.

I specialize in anti-aging advice.

What I do is help women over forty look like they are still in their thirties!

What makes me the best is that I've tried it all. My inexpensive tips and tricks have women raving about their youthful skins as far away as Sydney, Australia! Check out my website, where I have an e-book on these beauty secrets too! Feel free to share! And if you join my mailing list I give away free samples. Tell your friends!

As soon as I started my side hustle, I would introduce myself on every occasion as a life coach, not by my nine-to-five career. Make the elevator pitch automatic when you meet anyone new. Remember, it's meant to be someone's first impression! Make it short, snappy, and confident.

I like to keep in mind the old advertising acronym KISS. This stands for Keep It Simple, Stupid! Don't overcomplicate your pitch. Confused minds don't buy. Keep this tight! Make sure you get business cards printed for follow-up purposes, too. Services like Vistaprint make these a cinch to design and order, and they allow your elevator pitch to lead to concrete action. If the person you're introducing yourself to happens to have a need for exactly your service, you want them to be able to follow up with you easily!

Engage in Content Marketing

You may hear the term "content marketing" thrown around a lot. What is it? Simply producing and sharing valuable content, for free, with the intent to make a sale in the future—from how to style your hair with a beachy wave to how to whip up the perfect summer salad. Pure and simple. Consumers are spoiled for choice these days, so in order to appeal to them, earn their trust, and have them buy from you, you need to add value to their lives and have them get to know you by what you share. Whereas the elevator pitch depends on in-person encounters, content marketing casts a much wider net.

Whether it's through blog posts, video tutorials posted on YouTube, brief introductory webinars, free samples of a product, or a free introductory class, people want to "try before they buy." It's that straightforward. This approach builds familiarity and trust, but it's also where most people slip up. That's why the average blogger gives up after their first post—they get frustrated about the fact that they aren't famous or making money after five minutes. But guess what? As with any business, it takes time and consistency (and at least twenty blog posts) before anyone notices you.

The unfortunate thing is that most people are unaware of how to allocate their time when it comes to producing vs. promoting. They aren't aware that as amazing as their content is, it's important that people get to SEE IT.

Then, once you've laid a groundwork for attracting paying clients with great initial promotional content that drives traffic and grows credibility, keep in mind that your work and expertise are worth paying for! Teasers bring in your audience but won't pay the bills.

Advice on Pricing

Pricing is critically important! There are two main risks here: overpricing and underpricing.

If you overprice, you will hurt your sales, box clients out, and struggle to get crucial testimonials and have sufficient "wins" in your business. You will be inaccessible to your target audience.

But most common in side hustles is the opposite: underpricing.

If you underprice you will kill your margins and your product/service might appear "cheap." Many people equate price with value, so if you are too far on the lower end the assumption might be that your product or service is simply no good. Which is not true! It just means that sneaky impostor syndrome has got you too scared to raise your rate more in line with your market. You may fear that you aren't worth it, or question your right to take people's hard-earned money.

Nonsense! You're offering something special and unique. Most people don't understand the value of their time. Time IS money. Your time matters. Value it and others will too!

The best way to kick off your pricing is to know your competition: What is the going rate for your product/service on the market? How do you compare in terms of quality, expertise, and experience?

Research five to seven respected people or companies in your field. What do they charge? You don't have to use their exact rates, but knowing this information will let you peg a realistic target for your own earnings, even if it's something you build up to slowly.

I started by offering around half the normal going rate as a beginner. Then I increased in steady increments as my experience grew and there was more demand for my coaching. Don't feel that you can never raise prices! The more experience you have, the more you are worth. Plus, as you get busier with clients and new opportunities, your time becomes more valuable.

Important note: Don't have too many pricing tiers! I knew a life coach with six packages—the diamond package, the gold package, the starter package, and so on. It creates decision fatigue and makes people tired and confused before they even begin!

Stick with a premium and cheaper package, two options maximum, unless you have a specific need for offering extra. For example, if you are a coach, you can sell an e-book or one-on-one coaching. The e-book may be $9.99 and the coaching $99. The same goes for physical products and consulting. Have one lower-end and one higher-end offering. As a consultant, you might offer a strategic report (perhaps in the form of a subscription) or an ongoing consulting agreement. Do what works best for you—even if you balk internally at the price tag you're setting. Believe that you're worth it, and stand by your value.

I saw a great Instagram post once that said, "First they will ask you why you are doing it, later they will ask you how you did it." I hear this a lot. People were shocked I was leaving such a good career. And now they say: "The CEO of XYZ is paying you to advise them?! How do you even get that kind of work?" Or: "How did you get featured in X publication?" For too many people, putting themselves out there is so scary that they can't imagine anyone else doing it. But like anything else, with exposure you can conquer your fears—run a marathon, present to a large group of people, ask for a raise at work. You are in this for the long game, my friend. And your self-approval is all that counts. Doing work that matters to you is your only real obligation to yourself and to the world. You have the opportunity right now, no matter how late it might feel, to live your life the way that is true to you. That's well worth spreading the word about.

Soon enough people will want to know how you created such a killer side hustle too!

Over to you ✦ ✦ ✦ ✦ ✦ ✦ ✦ ✦

Think of one to three people who support and believe in you, no matter what. Think of these people in moments of doubt or when putting the word "out there" about your work. Try to borrow their confidence in yourself! Ask them to help you practice your elevator pitch, too.

Use that confidence to create a sample pricing structure. Then double-check that it covers the value of your time and doesn't sell yourself short!

Lastly, brainstorm how you can connect with your audience periodically through content marketing. What format/medium will you use to do this? What will the frequency be? The best content marketers go months without selling a single thing. It really solidifies the trust of their audience.

For instance, I send a free weekly confidence book to my beloved email subscribers—you can join at www.susie-moore.com to see how I do it. One email a week is all it takes to create a global, interactive community! Get started and watch your own mailing list grow.

11

What You Don't Know About Failure

"This may come as a surprise to you but failure is an illusion. No one ever fails at anything. Everything you do produces a result. Failure is a judgment. It's just an opinion."
  –Dr. Wayne W. Dyer, author of *Your Erroneous Zones*

"Worry is a way to pretend that you have knowledge or control over what you don't—and it surprises me, even in myself, how much we prefer ugly scenarios to the pure unknown."
  –Rebecca Solnit, writer

You already know I got fired in my early twenties. I'm not alone. Madonna, Oprah Winfrey, Walt Disney, Michael Bloomberg, and Mark Cuban all got booted from various jobs too. Yet we still stigmatize it.

Oh, rejection. The word alone stings. There is perhaps no greater human fear than being refused, denied, and dismissed, especially when we really care about what we have put "out there"—our hearts, our work, our ideas. As a writer, a former sales director for a Fortune 500 company, and, well, a human being, I have been rejected on many levels and under many circumstances. It never feels like a good thing, at least at the time.

What we often do not understand about rejection is that it is often simply temporary, sooner or later somehow helpful, or a simple course correction. The problem with rejection is not the rejection itself, but the fact that we cannot understand the greater plan behind it in that moment. Nor do we want to, as we are too busy licking our wounds and cursing the world. Rejection only makes sense with hindsight.

How many times in life have you looked back and realized the job, the love interest, the apartment was not meant to be yours, as something much better arrived afterwards? I can say "check!" to hundreds of these experiences. It makes me laugh (often with relief) now.

When I moved to New York I was interviewing everywhere and anywhere. I reached out to a lot of people to have coffee, share information, network. At the time (funnily enough) it was the most senior people who made time for me. Yet I spent my time foolishly being upset about the others who didn't! In the end I got the perfect job and stepping stone into the market. Those who rejected me made room for the right people who in the end hired me.

The truth is, when we are blown off, the vast majority of the time it is not even about us. The person who rejects us is simply focused on other qualities than those we have to offer. Additionally, what we perceive to be rejection is often not even actual rejection at all—just not the right timing. Mark Cuban was fired from his job at a computer store and that was the last day he ever worked for anyone else. Look at him now.

Rejection can simultaneously be the most awful blow and the most awesome wake-up call (and course correction). It can feel like the biggest disaster, especially when delivered—often very abruptly—when you're least expecting it. But actually, success and failure are on the exact same road—success is just farther down the path. And there is no such thing as a "wrong" path.

You may notice how often failure has come up in the course of this book—even though you're probably reading it because you want to succeed! There's a reason for that. It's critical we cover failure here, because make no mistake, you will experience some setbacks in your side hustle that may *feel* like failure, and it's important that you not let them discourage you for too long. (A little disappointment is natural, as long as it doesn't dampen your spirits permanently.)

Here are some of my more recent failures:

+ I neglected to include a simple link to my website from articles that were shared globally over 100,000 times. (People couldn't find me easily: a massive lost opportunity.) If you've spent any time working for an online business, you'll have a rough idea of how much potential business (through conversion) may have been lost here!

+ When the time came for me to create a website, I spent way too much on one with an outdated theme that I had to replace shortly afterwards because it wasn't secure and couldn't be updated (talk about pricey). You can create your own website via the free resources I have listed at the back instead of hiring one out. Many entrepreneurs have started profitable hustles with $0 and lots of heart!

✦ I wrote 70 percent of a book I decided I didn't like, so I didn't publish it. I realized that it sounded good to other people rather than felt good and authentic to me—oh, the hours spent!

✦ I created my first online product and told my partners it would be ready in April. It was ready in October.

I have done too much at once, or focused my energy in the wrong place. I have another partly completed course that I won't finish and multiple proposals that I won't send out simply because they are not the right thing for me right now. It has taken me a long time to realize that less with deeper focus is better. And only your intuition can guide you on what is right! So listen. And focus on one or two things at a time, maximum, as you are starting out. Add more once you start to catch your stride. You are already working a day job, so focus is critical in your side hustle hours!

Sure, I rue my wasted energy, hours, and lost cash. But it was all part of the learning curve and hey, in business, sometimes you lose a little money. That is why I recommend getting paying clients before creating business cards or a professional website—or anything that requires startup costs, in fact. You don't need them to get going with the first steps of creating your new gig.

This is another reason the side hustle is so awesome! You are already making money from your day job. You are in a better position to take a small financial hit if one happens, whether it's from a failed investment in a website design you don't like or if this year's holiday bonus turns out to be a disappointment.

"Ever tried, ever failed. No matter.
Fail. Fail again. Fail better."
—Samuel Beckett

A rejection story I like to retell happened with a big online publication that I really, really wanted to write for. I approached the editor multiple times, with no luck. About a month or two later, they randomly published some of my work, obviously through a syndication agreement they have with another publication I had written for.

This piece was shared many times and I had hundreds of new email subscribers to my weekly confidence boost as a result of this one republication. I thought to myself, "This is it! I'll approach the editor one more time and tell them that there is plenty more where that popular piece came from if they'd like me to write for them!" I emailed the editor. DENIED. Sometimes your fondest hopes just aren't going to become reality—but other opportunities are still out there. So press on! The sea is abundant with marine life even though you may have had your eye on just one catch. Go fish!

I love this passage from *The Success Principles* by Jack Canfield:

"Herbert True, a marketing specialist at Notre Dame University, found that:

- ✦ 44 percent of salespeople quit trying to sell to a prospect after the first call
- ✦ 24 percent quit after the second call
- ✦ 14 percent quit after the third call
- ✦ 12 percent quit trying to sell to their prospect after their fourth call

"This means that 94 percent of all salespeople quit by the fourth call. But 60 percent of all sales are made after the fourth call. This revealing statistic shows that 94 percent of all salespeople don't give themselves a chance at 60 percent of the prospective buyers. You might have the capacity, but you also have to have the tenacity! To be successful you have to ask, ask, ask, ask, ask!"

Amen, Jack.

Let me ask you this. What do you think that 94 percent would say if they were asked about their sales career? They would probably say they failed. But did they? Hells no. They just gave up too soon. In fact, as a coach nothing saddens me more than when a talented person gives up out of hopelessness or feeling like a failure. You never know how close the brink of a break could be. Woody Allen said that "80 percent of success is showing up." So show up!

Here is what you need to remind yourself of when you experience rejection in your side hustle. You are not alone. Anna Wintour was fired by *Harper's Bazaar*. "Everyone should be sacked at least once in their career because perfection doesn't exist," the

Vogue editor-in-chief told Alastair Campbell in his new book, *Winners: And How They Succeed.*

Oprah Winfrey was pulled off the air as an evening news reporter and was told that she was "unfit for TV." Michael Jordan was cut from his high school basketball team. Walt Disney was fired from a local newspaper when his editor told him he lacked imagination.

For me, getting fired made me realize what I am not suited to and made me assess what I am good at. My subsequent careers have been rewarding, fulfilling, and awesome. I needed the wake-up call to get out of what was a completely unsuitable job.

J. K. Rowling admits that her first *Harry Potter* book was rejected by twelve publishing houses. Twelve! When was the last time you attempted something that many times?

Here is what she said about failure in her Harvard commencement speech in 2011: "Failure in life is inevitable. It is impossible to live without failing at something, unless you live so cautiously that you might as well not have lived at all—in which case, you fail by default."

A lot of my readers write to me about this. You are afraid that you are not fulfilling your potential. You are scared that your life is wrong somehow. You feel as if you are betraying yourself and your calling every morning on your commute to work at a job that isn't aligned with your true goals.

This is a note I received from someone who is part of my online community:

"I recently moved to the U.S.A. with the hopes that I would have more opportunity and possibility to figure out what it is that I really want to do in life professionally. I have many interests and the thought of choosing any single one makes me a little sad because I feel like I would be neglecting all the others. I am currently working in a corporate setting while I try to explore during evenings and weekends."

Guess what? Your side hustle is the most practical, possible, and awesome opportunity to pursue your passions. You can follow them and really build something big from them. The only possible failure is not getting started. When you do nothing, as J. K. Rowling says, you fail "by default." Action is always better than inaction. Believe this and let it steer you towards harnessing your dormant talents and greatness. And in doing so you are going to have to do something really important: let go of (or rapidly reduce the influence of) what other people think. Derek of Greatist said to me when I asked him about how to get over the fear of failing,

"I'm not sure I ever did. I still feel those things. I just don't let it stop me. I let it fuel me and I see this as a big journey of learning. I'm confident. I'm hell-bent on building and making this difference that I want to make in the world. I won't allow anything to get in my way. I learn almost entirely by fucking things up first—and sometimes I have to fuck it up a couple times. I wish that wasn't true, but it's super true for me at least. I think success is really not about not making mistakes, but about (and this isn't my phrase) mistakes well handled."

How true! I never would have met my completely compatible husband unless I had the bad experience of my first marriage. Unless I got fired from my first job I would never have gotten started as a recruiter, which kicked off my decade-long successful sales career. Unless I truly hated my last boss I would not have had the courage to quit my corporate job and commit to working as a coach, writer, and consultant. Find the good in the failure. It's always there.

Over to you ✦ ✦ ✦ ✦ ✦ ✦ ✦ ✦

Think of a recent personal or professional failure. How can you use this experience as an opportunity to learn something about yourself? There is much value in failing! Don't let personal or professional setbacks negatively impact your outlook: reframe them as learning and growth opportunities!

12

How to Leverage Your Talent to Make Money

"What's easy to you is amazing to others."
–Derek Sivers, writer and entrepreneur

"The best way to do it is to do it."
–Amelia Earhart

When most of us think about our passion we rarely think of it making us money. Usually passion is something reserved for our leisure time, and not everything you are passionate about should be a revenue source—playing golf, teaching your dog new tricks, writing poetry, or selling vintage items on eBay might be activities you want to keep just for fun. Maybe you enjoy knitting more when you don't have a set output you have to meet, or you love attending yoga class but don't want the pressure of showing others the headstand pose you've not quite mastered. That's fine! If you are an incredible cook you might want to reserve your talents for people you love. You don't have to want to cook for others or teach others your culinary secrets. But if you do—think of how many people would love to learn how to cook, or the entire market out there that might enjoy your gastronomic creations. Martha Stewart started out as a local caterer. Bethenny Frankel baked and delivered her own cakes under the name Bethenny Bakes. You need to identify which passion you would like to make a business—one that can live and breathe and sustain itself and one that you won't resent as it grows and demands more of your creativity, time, and energy. Then—down to business!

The secret to success is being resourceful. The number one way to do this is to use your network. It's bigger than you think. As was covered in the previous chapter, don't be afraid to let your contacts know that you're open for business. Post your side hustle work on social media, share your elevator pitch with everyone you meet, and start an email list updating people with your offers. Most people will support you. After some time my corporate clients became some of my biggest supporters and even coaching clients (turns out a few had, or wanted to begin, their own hustles).

The following reinforces the point that hustles are differentiated from hobbies by producing income: So many of my coaching and consulting clients spend more time worrying about their website and business cards when they start out than they do about getting paying clients—but I started making thousands in extra monthly income BEFORE I had a website or a business card. Yes, they can be useful tools, but they're no substitute for your own hustling attitude.

I also could have procrastinated for years before writing this book, waiting for this interview or that interview to come through. I won't lie—I was slow in publishing this (six months behind schedule). But I pushed it out.

Here was the email I sent to my friends when I was looking for coaching clients. You can use this as the basis for your own outreach!

Hello friends!

Please forgive the mass email.

For those of you who do not know, I am currently attending New York University to get a certificate in Personal Coaching. I am now ready to take on some new clients (at a very affordable rate) for experience as I gain my certification.

It is preferable for me to coach people I do not know, so I am asking for your help in finding someone you might know who would be willing to engage in this exciting process with me. It is a 6-week engagement for an hour a week (on phone or in person). I am enthusiastic to work with people who are committed to drive positive change in their life.

I need to call any referrals by 11/18 for a 15-minute call to see if there's a good fit. If you could send me names/phone #'s of anyone that might be interested, please let me know as soon as possible.

Also, many of you already expressed interest in wanting to be coached as well. If so, please send me your most suitable contact information, as there might be classmates of mine that I can refer you to.

I am very passionate about this field and know it can be extremely rewarding for anyone!

Look forward to hearing from you.

Thanks so much—Susie

Start where you are with what you have. The trick to kicking off a successful side hustle in record time is to put word out—get orders or service requests and just BEGIN. It's a common misconception that you need a lot of money to start a business. Several people have said things to me along the lines of "Well, you had all of this money saved from a lucrative career, so it must have been easy for you to invest it into your business," but my initial set-up costs were precisely $0. In fact, I made it a condition of my side hustle that it had to pay for itself, so I had paying clients before I spent a cent on my business. I knew that if my side hustle were not self-sustaining, I'd never be able to grow it to a point that would allow me to quit my job without dipping into my savings.

You don't need an office or studio. You can help someone with their résumé over Skype or in a café, for example. You can show people how to housebreak their puppies in their apartment and in the park. You can be a freelance web designer and work from anywhere remotely. My friend Amber, a photographer and videographer, generates up to $4K a month for just the price of a latte or sandwich with a new client! Plus, she chooses when and how much extra work to take on. While she balances her demanding day job with her growing video business, Amber says, "I take frequent breaks and will step back from projects if I think they are weighing on me too much." She also makes sure to value herself properly by never working for free. While this can be a technique for getting your foot in the door, it's important to value what you're offering. That way, others will too.

Look around you. Who can you add to your email list? How can you grow this list? What did you leave untapped? Your volleyball group? Old coworkers? College alumni? The parents of your children's friends? What Facebook and LinkedIn groups are you in? Can your spouse help with his or her friends? Remember—the world needs your product or service, so you must not be bashful in sharing it!

While social media is great for building brand awareness, it's very noisy and can become quite expensive. The changing nature of the various algorithms each platform uses and ever-shifting user sentiment has meant that it's become increasingly challenging (and *more* expensive) to compete with already fully established influencers and brands.

I get it, having a big social media following is sexy, and there are people making big money in the Influencer Marketing sector with sponsored posts, images, tweets, and videos. It's a great space to play in if you can commit to keeping your social channels consistently up-to-date, on brand, and of value to others. If you're focused on a tech-savvy audience and have special design or photography skills, you may want to focus on your social media following first and foremost, whether on Snapchat, Pinterest, or Instagram (#goals). But for less visible side hustles, old-fashioned email outreach will be your best bet.

Interestingly, many U.S. marketing executives believe that email marketing contributes as much to their revenue as banner ads, their website, and all of their social media avenues altogether! Email has nearly three times the user base as Facebook and Twitter combined. And most social media marketing is aimed at email acquisition anyway—ever notice that? Your email address is coveted by businesses everywhere!

This is why building and nurturing a mailing list is so critical. Regardless of what happens in the social media ecosystem and which apps come or go, you have an incredibly effective way of communicating with your audience. This doesn't mean you should abandon all social media efforts, it just means that email marketing is still an incredibly powerful tool for your side hustle.

Here are just a few things you can do to build your list, social media presence, and brand:

✦ Extend an invitation to those already in your network (social media, personal email directory). Side note: always ask permission before adding people to your list, unless they sign up themselves.

✦ Be a guest presenter/blogger for another business, show, website, or blog and add a link for people to sign up to your site/newsletter. Most publications are totally fine with this unless there is a conflict of interest in your offering.

✦ Include a very apparent sign-up or opt-in page on your site. You will be surprised how even then many people who visit your site and love it will not sign up, so make it very visible.

✦ Create an "opt-in gift." Some people cringe when they hear this, but it is a fair trade. Someone gives you their email address? You give them something of value up front. Pay attention the next time you visit a website—they almost always want your email address and will often give you something in exchange. This might be a report on the latest stock trends or a free introductory video training to Krav Maga.

✦ Nurture your list and potential sign-ups. Assume that anyone on your list could be a potential client, business partner, or referral. Add incredible and consistent value via weekly or monthly emails before asking for anything in return. Again, most people struggle with this.

It may be hard to see, but even non-web-based businesses can benefit from building an online following. Using a hairdresser as an example, you may send out a monthly video tutorial or post your work regularly on Instagram, showing the latest hair trends or posting a tutorial on how to do a messy bun for a casual date. Adding this kind of value first leads to people saying, "Hey, I really like him/her. I want to support their studio/salon/class." Content marketing at work! It gets people comfortable and familiar with you as an authority on the subject and, over time, increases demand to hire you.

For instance, my friend Hannah helped edit the first draft of this book. She was a friend of a friend and as I began writing she helped me out here and there with great advice—how to work with PR teams to schedule a celebrity interview, how to have a killer opening line, and more. She's a pro. We met at a picnic in Central Park and became friends over our joint love of reading and writing. She is an excellent freelance editor/writer and one of her side hustles was helping me put this together! One time she even hired me as a life coach to run a vision board event for The Newswomen's Club of New York. We have hired each other a few times over the past couple of years. What does this tell you? People are everywhere. Get to know them. Always be cultivating your network! The benefit will accrue to both of you.

As an example, I met a great fellow coach and life strategist named Stephanie St. Claire online after reading her work and reaching out to her on Twitter. When she later moved to NYC, we became friends! It's wonderful meeting people who share things in common with you. I asked her what advice she would give to someone looking to become an entrepreneur. She told me truthfully:

"Give yourself two years to become fully financially self-sustaining. The first year is going to be all about you building a groundswell of clients and customers that trust you, remember you, and are slightly obsessed with you. You will do this by serving them in multiple ways through your writing, videos, free content you share with them on social, and through the letters you write to their inboxes. You almost have to untether yourself from the money and just keep giving.

"This drives everyone mad! They think they're doing something wrong or they have 'cheap' customers that don't want to buy their offerings. But all that is happening is that you are building trust and nurturing relationships. The scales tip at some point—and you have NO CONTROL over the timing of this, so please just surrender to that part. But one day you'll notice that you're working a lot less feverishly and the money you are making is double or triple what you were making in the early days. It's worth it!"

She is right. The people who have followed my free weekly wellness tips every Sunday for years now ask me for coaching constantly. New opportunities arise out of the woodwork when you just keep giving!

The Kick-ass Truth about Multiple Revenue Streams

One thing I tell many of my clients when it comes to starting their side hustle is to be conscious of having multiple revenue streams, particularly in the beginning. In the same way your hustle is a nice hedge against income uncertainty at your job, having multiple streams of income is also a hedge against the business cycle and changes in the demands of your clients. Remember this too: You never do your best work when you are desperate for cash. Once money becomes an issue, you are too stressed out to let the creative juices flow. The more income flowing your way, the more creative you can be and the more selectively you can receive new opportunities. That's a big reason the side hustle is so magical. So to protect your cash cushion, diversify!

As your business grows, having multiple revenue streams will also allow you to determine what areas you would like to focus on (from an enjoyment perspective) and what areas you should focus on (from a business perspective) and expand/contract accordingly.

Some income streams may even be passive, such as selling a product, e-book, or course online, or rental income from that property portfolio you have slowly started building. Or even being a referral source for others (and taking a commission from successful introductions like recruiters do).

Here are just some of the ways my business makes money (in no particular order):

- ✦ My blog, via Google ads
- ✦ 1:1 life coaching
- ✦ Group coaching
- ✦ Writing for large publications
- ✦ Being a referral partner for other businesses and coaches

+ Executive coaching, consulting, and advisory to startups
+ Selling my online courses, Side Hustle Made Simple and How to Get a Raise in 30 Days
+ This book!
+ Being a spokesperson on the topic of confidence for large companies
+ Hosting events such as vision board parties

There is a caveat here. While I was a full-time employee, I really only focused on #2 and #4 to avoid burnout. I added all additional sources of income thereafter. Start with one piece, then add more in as you go!

Before we wrap up this focus on finances, I want to share James Altucher's opinion of creating multiple revenue streams. His point of view that the path of taking a "safe" corporate job, funding a 401(k), and working for others for decades until reaching retirement is outdated has impacted my business and life immeasurably. Rather than following the traditional path of relying on historically low raises and salary growth, conservatively putting savings in a stock plan with high fees, and locking away money in a highly illiquid house with lots of unexpected maintenance costs, he proposes something radical: investing in yourself first.

As Altucher says:

"Unfortunately, incomes have been going straight down while inflation is going up. The average salary for people aged eighteen to thirty-five has gone from $36,000 in 1992 to $33,000 now and it's only getting lower.

"Meanwhile, the people I know who are doing the best financially have multiple streams of income, do not have a single job, and often the work they do is 100 percent related to their experience and not their education.

"'But what about the arts?' I get it. You can learn the arts and humanities in school. And you can have many social experiences in school. But the reality is, with $1.3 trillion in student loan debt (and rising), there are many other, cheaper, safer ways to learn these things. Ways that would be just as enriching, valuable for your future (even more valuable, since you will not have debt), and positive socially.

"Every society builds its 'religion' to keep the masses in check. All I'm saying is: Don't reject that religion. Maybe many of its tenets are good for you and your family and the people you love. But always be skeptical. Make sure that if the plane crashes, you are able to put the oxygen mask on your own face first. This is how you help the most people. By helping yourself. By choosing yourself."

I had to set aside a lot of received wisdom to leave my well-paying job at a big corporation when I went full time to my side hustle. Conventional wisdom says it's risky—but sometimes, listening to conventional wisdom is the riskiest step of all.

Over to you ✦ ✦ ✦ ✦ ✦ ✦ ✦ ✦

Do research on others who are doing the work in the world that you want to do. Look on their websites on their "Work With Me" tab or "Programs and Courses" section: What strikes a chord with you? You will likely find a whole lot of offerings within their business—in-person options to pay for time with them, books for sale, tickets to events they are hosting, iTunes downloads, and so on. Yoga instructors may offer retreats, individual sessions, and group classes, with the occasional free outdoors class in the summer as part of their content marketing. Pet groomers may charge extra for home visits and for different levels of pampering. Stylists can offer a one-time wardrobe consult or a more intensive closet decluttering intervention. Pay attention to what excites you and let the ideas inspire you. Remember—competition in your field is just proof there is a marketplace, and that is a great thing! Use it as market research and as inspiration. As you start your side hustle, which income stream do *you* want to focus on growing first?

BONUS: Collaborate with other hustlers and entrepreneurs at every opportunity. Find your tribe. The bigger your community, the more "luck" you will have. Who do you know that already does some similar work in the field you want to enter? Brainstorm a list and reach out by adding value to these people! The larger your network, the more people who will be interested in doing business with you later.

13

Why You Must Start Your Side Hustle:
The Spiritual Imperative

"It is better to live your own destiny imperfectly than to live an imitation of somebody else's life with perfection."

–The Bhagavad Gita

"Let the world know why you're here and do it with passion . . . Don't die with your music still inside you."

–Dr. Wayne W. Dyer

What does your life look like when you stand back and see the big picture? Imagine your eighty-year-old self lying in bed, considering the life you've had and all the choices you've made. The ancient Greeks used to "practice death every day." They would foster a wider perspective on their life daily and allow this to infuse all of their thoughts, actions, and behavior so as not to be driven by more petty concerns. South Koreans, meanwhile, attend their own mock funerals as a way to enhance their appreciation of being alive today. In her book *The Top Five Regrets of the Dying*, hospice nurse Bronnie Ware writes about how many of the patients she nursed in their final days regretted that they lived a life other people expected of them and not the life *they* truly wanted to live. By contrast, when we use our talents, skills, and gifts, we don't leave room for regret.

We all secretly know this. What bigger motivation can there be to pursue work that you really love? Bronnie herself became a palliative care professional when she felt that her life needed a deeper meaning. Some of us may seek for that purpose in volunteering or getting more involved with our faith, but others like Bronnie find a way to integrate their deeper purpose with their daily work.

Of all the people I coach, their finest hour is when they make the decision to bet on themselves. Choosing yourself means doing work that you love on your terms, not work that is tasked to you by a boss or expected from you by a figure of authority. When you step out of a structure that tells you what you do, you are in a position to choose what you want to do. This is what your free hours are for! It's your life—spend it on actions that feed you.

You choose. It's all you.

When you see the whole picture of your life it allows you to have a lot more perspective in your decision making. Steve Jobs said something in his 2005 commencement speech at Stanford University that still gives me chills every time I hear it:

"Remembering that I'll be dead soon is the most important tool I've ever encountered to help me make the big choices in life. Almost everything—all external expectations, all pride, all fear of embarrassment or failure—these things just fall away in the face of death, leaving only what is truly important. Remembering that you are going to die is the best way I know to avoid the trap of thinking you have something to lose. You are already naked. There is no reason not to follow your heart."

If there is an impact that you know you want to make on the world, that tugs on your heart, you have no choice but to start your side hustle. Having witnessed the amazing things that have happened for clients when they take the leap, I'm a true believer.

Choosing to turn your passion into a business is about shifting the purpose of your days from serving your boss to being your own boss. It's about getting the life you want. That means shifting your focus to take care of your needs before those of the people issuing your paychecks. One of the great things about making this change is that it doesn't just give you a new source of income. It gives you a new respect for your time and energy. After all, how can you succeed in your fledgling business if you're stressed or run-down? This is part of what makes jumping into a side hustle so rejuvenating. It gives you permission to make taking care of yourself your first obligation.

That's why Jason Wachob of mindbodygreen makes sure to meditate regularly: "Meditation has been game changing for me.

It helps me with stress, creativity, and focus." How She Made It founder Mary Keane-Dawson emphasizes the same thing, saying about meditation, "It's as important to empty your mind as it is to be fully in the present, at least once a day. By doing so you reboot and that allows you to reset and revisit your priorities on a daily basis." MNDFL founder Ellie Burrows is on the same page—unsurprisingly for someone whose side hustle was all about creating a meditation studio! Her first recommended step for hopeful entrepreneurs? "I would advise them to work on themselves before trying to work on a business. Human beings are very tribal and it does really take a village to do certain things. Getting help outside of yourself, whether that's in the form of a meditation teacher, therapist, spiritual adviser, life coach, or friend, can be very beneficial."

As it turns out, creating a business by starting a side hustle out of your passion (whether that's as a dating coach, a freelance designer, an interior decorator, or a financial advisor) is about more than money. It's about improving your life quality. Taking care of your vision. Fostering a sense of purpose. Getting out of the rat race. When you take your goals and talents seriously, you affirm your value. That means saying "no" to the forces that want you to give up on your quality of life to stay at the office longer, or to embrace deadening security over liberating freedom. Meditation and other types of self-care are a key piece of the puzzle, whether that's meditation, yoga, daily affirmations, journaling, whatever works! Don't forget that a commitment to your side hustle is a commitment to yourself. It's your job to look after Number One! Nurture your creative side with all the positive energy and kind acts of self-care that you can find.

One of my first coaching clients said to me, "Susie, when I'm at work at an ad agency, all I do (secretly) is pin fashion looks together and research vintage jewelry." Her passion was so obvious—she created lookbooks on the weekends, followed designers on Instagram, and always looked beautifully downtown chic on a pretty tight budget. She just needed to step back to realize it. And now, two years later? She works nights and weekends as a personal stylist and plans to transition to full time once she builds up her clientele.

Again—what is the worst that can happen? She won't like it. Clients will run dry. She will miss her old office environment and hate all the back-end work that a business entails (accounting, taxes, website management). So what? She will get another job just like her last one (that might even pay more).

And . . . what is the best that can happen? She becomes a successful CEO doing work she is completely obsessed with. She writes a book on style. She becomes best friends with top trend-setters; designers follow her on Twitter. She moves to Paris. She has celebrity clients and spends the winters in Los Angeles. She launches her jewelry line. Who knows? The possibilities are endless. "I dwell in possibility," Emily Dickinson wrote. Well, so does my client. And so can you—but only if you begin.

I was speaking to a friend recently who was asking me how much I work. It gave me pause because I no longer consider this question in my life. When I was employed I used to resent being in the office after 5 p.m. or arriving home late after a business flight and missing dinner with my husband. My answer surprised her (and me). I said, "Well, my calendar is always full, but I never feel like I'm working." I thought that was pretty cool! It was like a little wink from the universe that I am doing the right thing. Busy but never *working*. What could be better than that?

Over to you ✦ ✦ ✦ ✦ ✦ ✦ ✦ ✦

Write a letter from your eighty-year-old self. Start, "Dear Me, I am so happy that in my life I wasn't afraid. I am so thankful that I . . ."

Then, write down all the things you secretly want to do from the vantage point of your older self.

Here are some good questions to keep in mind as you start a conversation with this wiser, older version of you. Ask yourself:

- ✦ What do I really, really, really want?
- ✦ Where am I holding back?
- ✦ What will I congratulate myself for having the courage to do, right now?
- ✦ What part of myself do I really need to honor and be true to (even if this goes against others' expectations of me)?
- ✦ What really makes me feel happy and alive?
- ✦ How can I make my happiness and my truth my number one priority?

Don't hold back. Allow everything to come to the surface, even if it's scary. This can go beyond your work and the impact that you make with it. But I know pursuing work that you love will be up there.

14

Why You Must Start Your Side Hustle:
The Practical Perks

*"Do what you have to do until you
can do what you want to do."*
–Oprah Winfrey

"Well . . . Why not me?"
–Mindy Kaling, actress and author

OK, so we've covered the inspirational side of things. Now let's get into the nitty-gritty. Hopefully we feel pretty convinced that given our limited time on earth, and the tremendous untapped talent and creativity we know we have lurking within us, we have to satisfy the inner stirring we are feeling to make more of our lives. We need to seize it, nurture it, and see what can happen. It's unhealthy not to. But there's a practical argument for doing it too, as previous chapters on creating income streams should have tipped you off. Let's recap!

Here are some key reasons:

✦ You hedge against an uncertain economy—there is no such thing as job security anymore.

✦ You earn more money—so yes, you can feel good about your daily $4 latte, pay off some debt, or go on that holiday.

✦ You learn new skills that are critical in this era—for example, sales, marketing, negotiation, networking, WordPress, how to create a CRM system for your clients (that's customer relations management, for those not in the know), as well as basic accounting and taxation guidelines. Skills that may benefit you in your day job too, until you no longer need it!

✦ Set-up costs can be totally minimal—I started life coaching with no website, business cards, or office. I charged $100 per hour, met people through my own network (LinkedIn, Facebook), and met clients in coffee shops or over Skype rather than in an office of my own. I also managed to convince my company to cover the costs of my coaching studies. If you speak up and ask, you can uncover budgets you didn't know existed!

✦ You can totally work it around your schedule— nights and weekends are all yours to use, plus the hours you can use are immense when you realize that capacity is a state of mind.

◆ Online resources make it even harder to find excuses—you can contribute as a freelancer for 99designs, Fiverr (I was just reading about a woman who makes $9,000 a month—initially a side gig—doing voice-overs), Upwork, and Freelancer.com, which offer gigs from website bio writing to book cover design and language translation.

◆ You save money! Think about it. Time you spend building your business is time you are not at the bar, at the sample sale, at the four-hour lunch, or online shopping for ballet flats or golf clubs.

◆ You can tell your boss you're outta there one day down the line because your side hustle dough matches (or exceeds) your salary.

◆ You might invent/write/build the next greatest thing that people need.

◆ The opportunities are truly unlimited, unlike your (probably) limiting career. No glass ceilings or salary caps here!

If you're still not convinced, be aware that Sara Blakely created Spanx while selling fax machines full time (and only when Spanx became one of Oprah's favorite things did she resign from her job). Khaled Hosseini wrote the best-selling book *The Kite Runner* while working full time in a hospital. Michael Burry pursued his hobby of financial investing in between shifts at Stanford Hospital as he finished his residency. He left medicine shortly after to pursue his side hustle full time, starting a hugely successful hedge fund, making hundreds of millions of dollars by correctly calling the subprime mortgage crisis—he was the star of Michael Lewis's book *The Big Short* and was portrayed by Christian Bale in the movie of the same name.

Think you don't have what it takes to be that successful? Think again. Elizabeth Gilbert, author of *Eat Pray Love*, is a big mentor of mine (although she doesn't know it). In an interview with *Cosmopolitan* she said:

"I am 46 now, and I look back at the people who I was hanging out with in my 20s, and there were some who had what looked to me at the time like infinite power and infinite promise and infinite possibility. And they never did anything with it. And then there were other people who I kind of dismissed and thought didn't have anything—and then those people just blew my mind with what they ended up creating. To me, the most boring question in the world is, 'Who has talent?' and, 'Who doesn't have talent?' Because I have seen that that is not really where it's at. We will never know. There is no objective measure that we could use to tell who is talented and who isn't talented. You can only tell by what they make and what they make of their lives. I don't know how much natural talent I have. I know that I work harder than anybody I know. . . . In my 20s . . . I was a bartender, I was a waitress, and I worked in a bookstore. More important is work ethic and willingness to go after your goals.

"And you know, my first two books were written when I had three jobs. So sometimes when I hear people say, 'I would love to do this but I don't have time!' Or, 'Well, I have a real job and I would have to quit my job to write a book,' what I hear is that they aren't committed enough."

How will *you* step up your commitment? Once I was having brunch with two young women who are sales directors in the online advertising sector. Both are brilliant and successful. One of them shared with me an idea that she has about launching an event planning business specific to a particular industry. The concept sounded great. But let me let you in on a little secret. Ideas are overrated. A good-enough idea acted upon is better than a tremendous idea only talked about over waffles and mimosas.

As soon as she shared it she started poking holes in it: "Well, I want to move out of New York one day so it won't be sustainable," and "I don't really have any experience in the hospitality sector." Ah, here you are again, our old friend fear. I wanted to scream—Are you kidding me? You are a saleswoman! You make deals happen and close against all odds in one of the most competitive spaces of all time!

I know that in her day job she contacted a client upwards of 20 times in order to secure just one 30-minute meeting. You think this young woman could not get a few venues to talk to her and pitch her ideas the same way she does every working day of her life? And doesn't every city in the country have some kind of event, every day? And so I asked her (and you must ask yourself this too when your doubts creep in):

✦ *"Well, how might it work if you believed that it could?"*

✦ *"What skills do you have that would work in your favor here?"*

✦ *"How could it succeed in a way you have not necessarily thought of?"*

With those three questions this talented young woman solved her own problem. She realized, "I *am* a salesperson. I know how to persuade people. I know how to pitch ideas. I would just do my research (ding, ding, ding!) and tailor it to a new market!"

Fait accompli, my friends.

Now that she's had this insight, she's on the path to creating life how she wants it. What might that look like for you? Champions Of The Web CEO Dan Kolansky has done this with his side income from his business building company websites and online marketing campaigns. As he says, "It allows my wife to stay home with the kids and funds my love of hobbies like photography and camping. Long term, I want to build up to personal financial freedom and get the chance to spend the majority of my time with my family and on community-building in my area. Ironically, my business has gifted financial freedom to several of my clients already. Time to do it for myself."

Taking responsibility for your work, your income, and your hours on earth brings a lot of confidence into your life. It astounds me how many people feel their corporate skills— or any experience they have from years of working—are not transferable to a side business. I'm here to tell you that a lot of what you know from your professional life can be used in other valuable ways, too.

Not to mention that your side hustle will give you a stronger negotiating position with your day job. As Dan observes, "Your income isn't capped and neither are your horizons. If you don't like your job for some reason you can just tell them to pound sand and move on with your life. It also makes you more valuable to your job. If they know that your side gig is giving you equal or more income then the power in the relationship moves to you. They need you and you don't need them. This makes it very easy to ask for special treatment, extra vacation, raises, or the like . . . it has given me confidence in communicating with my boss (which actually improved our relationship)." Improving in one area of your life always improves others!

If you haven't already read *The Alchemist* by Paulo Coelho, I'll share one of its key insights: "All things are one." In other words, there are no isolated life skills or experiences we go through that do not help us in our future experiences. Even the boring parts of our past jobs (for me it was data entry and tracking revenue in an Excel spreadsheet) may teach you an important lesson that you can bring to your new business. It's all intertwined. This can also be a great opportunity to pick up new skills, which will only make you more flexible for any future ventures. Have a great idea for an app, but held back by your fear of coding? Sign up for a free tutorial online and you won't just get access to the ability to create your own digital products—you'll have a whole new area of expertise to add to your résumé and make you more well rounded. Maybe your new programming abilities will make you suddenly eligible for a promotion into a new role or department in your day job, but no matter what, it makes you more marketable, more self-confident, and less held back by seeming impossibilities. "I don't know how" is never the final answer—if other people can do it, you can learn how too!

Part of side hustling is always learning and improving yourself, so that you'll be prepared for any opportunities or challenges that come your way. Otherwise, your career and your sense of excitement about life will stagnate.

What do you have to lose? You are keeping your day job. Your rent continues to be paid. Your day job continues to support you in the same way it always has. You still have health insurance. As NatureMapr CEO Aaron says, by creating your own venture "You have reduced your level of risk, you don't need to dilute your company and take external investment, and you can do it on your own terms. You are your own boss."

Some other major practical benefits of the side hustle include:

✦ Setting your own hours. This is particularly great for parents/caretakers/travelers. . . . What could having control of your week/month/year look like for you? How could this help not only you, but the people around you? Maybe you would work for three hours in the afternoon while your child naps or goes to part-time day care.

✦ The opportunity to pay down debt or save for a specific goal using additional income. If you made an extra $500, $1,000, $5,000 per month—what would this money allow you and your family to do?

✦ Harnessing new skills and increasing your level of attractiveness in any future job searches. Having a side business is a great way to pursue a new career by dipping your toes in the water of a different field. It can also empower you to leave a bad boss once you're generating sufficient cash and are ready to take the big leap.

✦ Creating a buffer against layoffs or job loss. What freedom and opportunities will your new cash flow and business skills create for you if the stuff hits the proverbial fan this year, next year, in five years?

But sorry, reruns of *Homeland* won't support your long-term goals. You have work to do. So let's get started. Commit to earning supplementary income, and establish a monetary target and goals to establish accountability. That means getting down to details! When will you get your first client? What expenses will your side hustle cover for you? Setting concrete financial benchmarks will help keep your eyes on the prize as you build your new business. Create a schedule for each milestone you hope to achieve, and track your progress. Are you with me?

Over to you ✦ ✦ ✦ ✦ ✦ ✦ ✦ ✦ ✦

Again, ask yourself these questions about your hustle idea:

- ✦ How many hours a week can I devote to building this business?
- ✦ What connection can I leverage or what influencer can I reach out to for my next step forward?
- ✦ What does my monthly billing need to be to replace my current earnings from salary, plus make up for lost benefits?
- ✦ What skills do I have that would work in my favor here?
- ✦ How could it succeed in a way I have not necessarily thought of?

15

The Possibilities Are Endless

"Man often becomes what he believes himself to be. If I keep on saying to myself that I cannot do a certain thing, it is possible that I may end by really becoming incapable of doing it." –Mahatma Gandhi

"Without leaps of imagination or dreaming, we lose the excitement of possibilities. Dreaming, after all, is a form of planning."
–Gloria Steinem

Here is a little universal truth that not everyone is aware of. When you walk in the direction of your dreams, take action, get busy, and gain momentum, the universe greets you halfway. Steven Pressfield in his book *Do the Work* calls this "assistance." It is very, very real. You may have come across it elsewhere as positive thinking or the law of attraction, but the benefits accrue no matter the name. Without diminishing the real problems we all face in life, this elevates the importance of our own attitude towards our circumstances.

To encourage you to commit to your own dreams, I'll share some examples of how assistance has come to my aid in the past—not once, but many times. The key is to be open enough to see it! In June 2012, I was feeling a little bored and uncomfortable at work but had not yet started side hustling. I wasn't really aware that you could strike out on your own, and I was not sure how to begin or what I would do. I was also afraid that my boss would get upset if my focus was not 100 percent on selling advertising technology. (You'll be happy to hear that this is increasingly untrue. Unless you are under a strict contractual obligation, many employers actually support creative pursuits outside of work, with government employers as the major exception.)

Around that time, one of the co-founders of the startup I worked for called me out of the blue about an opportunity. He asked if I was interested in working in D.C. for the remainder of the year to see if I could generate some political advertising revenue. To this day I am not sure why he asked me, but I like to think that he saw me as someone who got results and was open to new projects.

This was unlike anything I had ever done before. As a native Briton, I had absolutely no understanding of the U.S. political system. Nada. Zip. Zero. All I knew at that point was that Obama was running again—I was not even sure who the Republican rival was! So not only did I give myself a crash course in U.S. politics, I watched CNN like an addict and read *Politico* like it was going out of style to fill in the gaps in my knowledge.

Then, between June and November, I spent the majority of my time in Washington, D.C., selling video campaigns to political action committees and advertising agencies. My new title was Political Sales Director and my second home became the W Hotel opposite the White House. Taxi drivers in D.C. recognized me. "Back to the W?" one asked while I was rushing into his car on my phone with my high heels and small suitcase, taken aback that he knew my destination.

I worked that unique, difficult-to-penetrate, and highly complex market like my life depended on it. One night I even had two steak dinners back to back—one at 6:30 p.m. and another at 9 p.m.—to accommodate two different client schedules.

My boss said he would have been "thrilled" if I generated $500K in advertising dollars. By November 3, 2012, when the last voting polls closed on the West Coast, I had generated almost $3 million. What is the moral of this story? I should carve my niche as a political expert? No. I had found my calling in Washington? Certainly not. The moral is this: You don't need to fit whatever preconceptions people think or tell you are needed to achieve something awesome.

I had no political background. I wasn't even a U.S. citizen who could vote. This was my first time selling media campaigns. I had no reason to succeed apart from a belief that I could and an unwavering work ethic. As Mindy Kaling likes to say, "Why not me?"

Making that experience rock (and earning a sweet little bonus from it—another lesson learned, *always* be asking for more) showed me what you can do in a short amount of time with massive application and belief. And get this: The biggest deal I closed—around $800K or so—came from an off-chance tip from a new connection I had made.

I had a last-minute meeting on my way back to New York with a small firm I had not heard of before and almost couldn't make it work. But I felt called to go. This was not one of the meetings I had slaved to secure. It was a little universal wink and blessing—a reward for my hard work and dedication. When you get busy, the universe—always unpredictably but with more fervor than you can imagine—meets you halfway and overdelivers. I have heard endless stories like this. This I know for sure. So often we don't give the universe the opportunity. We give up too soon or we don't even begin.

When this massive deal closed my boss bought champagne for the whole New York office and emailed a photo of me opening the bottle to the entire company. It was pretty freakin' awesome. I felt like a rock star. That year I won one of the five company awards they gave out at the holiday party for the entire global team in San Francisco. The irony was I was in Turks and Caicos with my husband and could not even accept it! I felt like one of those ballers who could not accept their VMA because they are on a shoot or doing something cool in a remote part of the world. Hey, a girl can dream, right?

There was yet another time the universe rocked for my husband Heath and me when we really needed it. Heath is the reason we live in the U.S. His hard work landed us in New York after his company transferred him here when he was twenty-three, when he also negotiated (and landed) green cards for us. Anyone who has gone through the green card process knows it is a very long and arduous one.

We love living in the U.S. more than anything else. So Heath (with massive universal assistance) secured our green cards via his firm. After seven years at one company he was ready to find a new role better suited to his long-term goals. He had really stuck it out for us over the years and embarking on a job search in a really competitive market felt overwhelming. Also, after seven years with an Australian company and an Australian work culture it's natural to feel a bit anxious about changing to work for a big American company. But, the universe helped out once again.

I was on a business trip in Miami. The trip was rescheduled twice because of my client's schedule and we ended up staying at the Viceroy Hotel, after we almost stayed at a different hotel—there are plenty of variables at work here, which is why you just have to trust the universe! Heath decided to join me and stay for the weekend.

We chose to have dinner at the hotel and, as I was ready before him, I headed down to the bar to grab a martini. I sat down just as the man next to me was presented with his meal, which looked delicious. I asked him what he ordered and we got talking about the menu. When Heath arrived we were chatting about things to do while visiting Miami, plus a little bit about our backgrounds— the usual stranger small talk. Only it turns out the man was a managing director and business head at one of the companies Heath really wanted to work for. Two weeks later, he was hired due to that serendipitous connection. Talk about a slam dunk!

Think about it—the date, the hotel, the timing at the bar, the open seat: everything conspired to make this happen for my husband. Luck? I don't think so. There is always a greater power at work than we can see or understand.

Here is my final story about the universe being on your side. I quit my job in December 2014. It was a big and scary decision, but after almost 18 months of side hustling (and averaging around $4,000 a month doing it) I was tired. I didn't have a good rhythm with my boss. We'd just moved into a new apartment and something told me I would be safe if I took the leap to work for myself full time in this new setting. It was terrifying but it also felt like I didn't really have a choice. This was my chance to show my faith, practice what I preach, and take the risk. After all, as I used to ask myself when I needed the boost, "Hey, what if it *does* work out?"

The first month going full time in my hustle was really hard. It was winter and Heath left the house every morning just after 6 a.m. I was alone and felt terribly selfish and guilty. I busied myself with writing and booking new clients, but leaving a corporate career after more than a decade was no easy transition. I had no fellow entrepreneurial friends. Everyone else was at work all day. And what was I doing? I looked at my closet full of blazers and heels and it sounds silly, but I felt like I no longer had a use for these things that made me feel important. I felt scared, uncertain, and I second-guessed myself a lot. Had I done the right thing? I gave up a big income in a booming industry. I lived in one of the most expensive cities in the world. Having come from such a poor family, part of me could not believe my actions. Was I stupid?

I flew to the U.K. to visit my mother and came back sad and scared. It should have been an exhilarating time but big change is tough. There is no sugarcoating it.

That lasted about a month. I did my usual LinkedIn updates and responded to recruiters, telling potential employers that I was not interested in full-time positions (feeling unsure and heavy as I did so). And then I had an idea. I wondered if anyone would consider hiring me as a consultant/adviser/coach to help build their business?

I could package my life-coaching skills, sales expertise, and general business experience and use it to advise senior management at high-growth Silicon Valley startups. (D.C. is full of consultants and I had learned what they do and how they work.)

The first two people I shared this idea with met me for coffee. They both wanted to hire me as an adviser for their businesses. I could not believe my luck! Thanks, Universe.

I'm not telling you these stories to gloat. I'm telling you because I want you to know that there are more incredible opportunities around us than we realize, if we remain proactive, receptive, and open. Even if you are introverted—remember: You are living in the best time on earth because the Internet is your best friend. You can speak to anyone, anytime, anywhere from the comfort of your sofa without seeing a soul or even opening your mouth. I have "friends" in entrepreneurial Facebook groups all over the world I am now getting to do business with who I will likely never meet, nor necessarily even speak to via Skype.

Challenge your own perception about what is possible for you. It doesn't take much to leave a comment on an Instagram photo or tweet an influencer that you like. Over time, these people will get to know you! So don't be afraid! It's just social media, and you never know where it could lead. Use the method of approach that fits your personality, and don't assume there aren't any options!

In times of doubt, guard your thoughts like a bulldog. When doubt creeps in, defer to why it WILL work out. I still have a list in my phone of why things will work out for me in any time of my life. They include people who will always hire me, as a back-up plan, a reminder of the size of my awesome online community and my supportive husband and friends.

I've been obsessed with self-help books since I was a kid and my mom and I would scour secondhand shops for good books at a good discount. Now I am the author of a self-help book.

So, time strapped? Start anyway. Not sure what your passion is? Start anyway. Self-doubting? Start anyway. I got you. Put all doubt, fear, and anxiety aside—just for a second—and ask yourself, "What if it *does* work out?"

Then buckle up. Take a deep breath.

And be prepared for it to come true.

Why Start a Hustle?

You really wanna know why?

It's not for the money. It's not to be a CEO of something. It's not to have full creative control or to one day hand in that overdue resignation letter.

It's 'cause you have to.

'cause you are good enough.

'cause you matter.

'cause your contribution matters.

Yes, I can give you tips and tricks and shortcuts that hopefully save you some frustration, assure you that you are not alone on this journey, and hopefully make your long nights at your laptop, studio, or workshop a little easier. But what is more important than the structure, the advice, the wisdom from others gathered here? Your inner wisdom. The wisdom that's compelling you to create something. That whisper that pushes you forward, the one that won't let up even when you feel down. The voice that urges you to forge ahead.

Honor that wisdom. It's not wrong. It asks you, "Hey, what if it *does* work out?"

So let's find out.

~ ~~THE END~~ ~
The Beginning . . .

Appendix

My Resource Bible

One of the amazing benefits of working in tech for so many years was that I came across so many different peer-to-peer web-based marketplaces that make it easy for aspiring entrepreneurs and side hustlers to hang out their shingle. From dog sitting to providing legal advice or guided tours, never before has it been so easy to put your product/service in front of millions of prospective customers.

Many of these platforms allow you to set up and promote your business *before* you make your first dollar. And given that many of us have multiple passions, promoting our work on several of these allows us to set up multiple revenue streams for our hustle. There really is no excuse; it has never been easier to get started. These are just some of the hundreds of platforms available and are a great way to get the entrepreneurial juices flowing.

Are You Secretly a Graphic Designer?

There are so many opportunities to offer your services online in the design space, from building websites to designing books/

magazines, business cards, packaging, and signage! In fact, I used 99designs to design this book cover and interior and I found my website developer on Fiverr.

99designs (99designs.com)—This hugely successful crowd-sourcing marketplace for graphic designers allows designers to read a prospect's brief and then compete for the business by providing preliminary design ideas. The prospect will then narrow down to a few designs/designers, fine-tune the brief, and select a winner, who can make anywhere from a few hundred to a few thousand dollars, depending on the project. Other platforms include **DesignCrowd (designcrowd.com)** and **crowdSPRING (crowdspring.com).**

Fiverr (fiverr.com)—Another huge marketplace for creative professionals. With Fiverr, you set an initial price of $5 and work upwards, depending on additions made to your offering or upselling. There are many success stories of people making thousands of dollars a month offering an array of services, from graphics and design to digital marketing, writing, translation, video, animation, music, audio, advertising, and more. I read a fascinating story on Business Insider about a former musician who started doing voice-overs for $5 apiece on Fiverr—he then started to experiment with video and was able to create more lucrative packages. Long story short, he has since quit his full-time job, paid off $50,000 in debt, and makes up to $23,000/month from what started as a side hustle!

Upwork (upwork.com)—Similar to Fiverr, Upwork provides a marketplace for web and mobile developers, designers and creatives, accountants, consultants, virtual assistants, translators, and copywriters.

Boost Media (boostmedia.com)—If you are a skilled copywriter, Boost Media may be a great platform for you.

Are You a Subject Matter Expert?

This actually comes as a surprise to many of the clients that I coach, but chances are you are already an expert in at least one area, whether that be your full-time job, your side hustle, or simply something that interests you. You can monetize that! There are so many avenues you can take to make money as a consultant. When I first transitioned from side hustling to full-time entrepreneur, I consulted (and still do) for a company by the name of Gerson Lehrman Group (GLG), who would pay me to speak with various corporations about digital media and programmatic advertising. This added a fantastic additional revenue stream.

Gerson Lehrman Group (GLG) (glg.it)—An American expert network based in New York that acts as a knowledge brokerage between corporations and business leaders, scientists, academics, former public-sector leaders, and subject matter specialists.

Guidepoint (guidepoint.com)—Much like GLG, they connect subject matter experts from more than a hundred industry categories across many sectors: Healthcare, Tech, Financial and Business Services, Consumer Goods and Services, Media and Telecom, Energy, Industrials and Basic Materials, and Legal and Regulatory. Similar platforms include **The Expert Institute (theexpertinstitute.com)** and **Popexpert (popexpert.com)**.

Do People Love Your Cooking?

You go, Martha Stewart! You can monetize that! This concept was completely unfamiliar to me until our good friend Chris, who is an amazing host and cook, introduced us to the concept of being paid to host dinners for complete strangers in their house, in your house, or at an independent venue. Whether you are an actual chef, an aspiring chef, or someone who simply loves to cook for people, there are a number of platforms that allow you to set your menu, time, location, number of people, and price! This could be the perfect first step for you to pursue that restaurant/hospitality dream.

Feastly (eatfeastly.com)—I have heard of people—from great home cooks to Michelin-starred chefs—earning thousands a month from this site.

EatWith (eatwith.com)—Similar to Feastly, EatWith currently has more than 500 people hosting dinners in 150 cities in 30 countries. To date, it has hosted more than 10,000 dinners. You can become a part of the action.

BonAppetour (bonappetour.com)—A slightly different platform that connects local home chefs with travelers, providing them with a unique experience.

CookUnity (cookunity.us)—Think Blue Apron meets Feastly. Based in New York City, CookUnity will give you use of their kitchen space, the best ingredients, and packaging and will help you market and distribute meals to foodies. Share your family recipes and your story and build a following.

Love to Paint? Fancy Yourself as an Artisan?

The Internet is bursting with opportunities for aspiring artists and artisans to promote, sell, and even loan their work! You can connect with buyers without having a pretentious gallery owner following them around and judging their ability to come up with the dinero. I have used some of these sites a number of times to browse for anything from wall art for our apartment to linen curtains. These platforms also provide a much cheaper alternative to setting up a retail location or even a market stall. (I once had a market stall in Sydney; it was an abnormally cold summer day and it was raining sporadically. I had already paid the nonrefundable fee of $250 to reserve my plot, so I said "screw it" and set up shop anyway—I sold $150 worth of product—suffice to say the economics of that day didn't work in my favor. Plus I finished the day drenched.)

Etsy (etsy.com)—A hugely popular global marketplace that connects buyers and sellers of unique goods both on- and offline. The marketplace, with its 24 million active buyers, is a behemoth for creators of anything from clothing to accessories, jewelry, art, crafts, and home goods. Etsy takes a transaction fee of 3.5 percent, but the platform provides tools and support that make it super easy to promote your product. Similar to Etsy, Zibbet (zibbet.com) is also worth looking at.

Ravelry (ravelry.com)—Love to knit or crochet? Ravelry allows users to upload their self-created patterns for purchase.

Redbubble (redbubble.com)—An artistic marketplace that connects buyers and sellers of anything from art prints to calendars, canvas prints, phone cases, T-shirts and hoodies, greeting cards, and more.

TurningArt (turningart.com)—A fantastic platform that allows artists to rent their work to businesses and homes. Leases can be renewed or the work can even be purchased if still available.

Are You a Natural Caregiver?

If you are a natural caregiver, whether it be babysitting, caring for the elderly, or pet sitting, there are a few great options.

Care.com—This is essentially a one-stop shop for caregivers to provide their services. From babysitting, to caring for children with special needs, the elderly, or dogs (walking, sitting, grooming, training), to house sitting, Care.com has done a great job of providing a marketplace, with 19 million members in 16 countries.

DogVacay (dogvacay.com)—Available across the USA and Canada, DogVacay connects pet owners with more than 25,000 caring sitters. The platform takes care of the administrative side, handling insurance, payment, and customer support so that you can just focus on taking care of the animal(s).

Rover (rover.com)—Rover is another, similar pet service. In fact, I read a *New York Post* article stating that, on Rover's platform, full-time sitters average $3,300/month, part-time sitters average $900/month, and those with a couple of stays a month average $250. This could be a perfect side hustle for retirees, freelancers, stay-at-home parents, or even teachers on summer break.

Talkspace (talkspace.com)—Talkspace has helped therapy adapt to the digital age and allows licensed therapists to speak with clients via smartphone or the web.

Know Your City Well? Speak Another Language?

Great side hustle opportunities there! My sisters all live abroad. One in Munich, one in Rome, one in Sabah (Malaysia), and one in Surrey, England. The sister in Munich speaks five languages and the one in Rome has lived there for many years and speaks beautifully fluent Italian. While they seldom allow me to lecture them about their side hustlin' potential, they do appreciate that there is a market for their skills. If you are passionate about your city, or linguistic skills, one of these may be for you!

GetYourGuide (getyourguide.com)—You can become a tour guide in your city/region and get paid to do it!

Vayable (vayable.com)—The website sums it up in one sentence: "Discover and book unique experiences offered by local insiders." Anything from offering a food crawl in Rome, to a nighttime photography tour in Paris, to scouting for street art in San Francisco, to showing people around the hottest spots in New York City's East Village; these are just some examples of what people have offered on their site. You list an experience and, if approved, you get the opportunity to make money. Heck, list several if it brings joy!

Verbling (verbling.com)—According to their site, there are 800,000 language learners and 37 languages being taught!

Looking briefly at the site, I noted that teachers appear to be earning anywhere from $10 to $40 an hour based on the pricing they set. The great thing about Verbling is that you can display your schedule and availability online, to avoid any back-and-forth.

Verbalplanet (verbalplanet.com)—Like Verbling, Verbalplanet is a peer-to-peer language site that allows you to set your schedule and rates and earn reviews. Based on a look at the site, $15–$25 appears to be a reasonable price point for a 45-minute lesson and some of the instructors on the platform have given thousands of lessons.

Feeling Geeky or Teachy?

Whether you are a full-stack engineer, a talented coder, great with tech support, or simply someone who likes to teach or tutor people on an array of subjects, there is a marketplace for your skills.

HelloTech (hellotech.com)—If you are the sort of person that has a knack for computer installation/repair, network setup, video game tech support, TV and audio support, or smartphone/tablet tech support, then HelloTech may be a great way to earn some extra cash on the side.

Catalant (gocatalant.com)—This is an impressive service that pairs MBA students and grads, who could not typically afford a big-name consulting firm, with business owners to assist with research and projects. Catalant takes a 14.5 percent cut, but some of the stories I have read have been really impressive, including one woman who left her job and, after doing several projects through Catalant, landed a three-week gig with a multinational company that paid $55,000 to have her help them analyze and redesign their financial process.

Codementor (codementor.io)—Codementor allows you to put your coding skills to use by pairing you up with those that need some one-to-one help. As a mentor, you would typically charge at least $10 for a 15-minute consultation on the platform, and there are people charging much higher.

Studypool (studypool.com)—This platform allows students to instant-message a tutor 24/7 and has helped more than one million students. Tutors can set their schedule as to when they are available to help answer homework questions, and top earners have exceeded $70,000 in earnings.

Wyzant (wyzant.com)—Much like Studypool, this online and in-person tutoring platform matches students and tutors across a broad spectrum of subjects and grade levels. Doing a quick search in my postcode for calculus (yuck!) tutors, I saw a range in pricing, from college students and recent grads charging $50/hour to lecturers/faculty/professors charging $200/hour, with many of them having received hundreds of ratings.

Prefer to Work In Person?

Let's face it, not all hustles can be done with a webcam and a Skype account, but there are still plenty of fantastic peer-to-peer marketplaces that match buyers and sellers of services that are delivered/performed in person.

TaskRabbit (taskrabbit.com)—A huge marketplace where you can promote your hustle in anything from handyman services to shopping and delivery, cleaning, moving help, or administrative services. "Taskers" can set their own prices and schedules. Looking at the site, I found people charging from $10 to as much as $150/hour. Australia has a similar site in **Airtasker (airtasker.com)**, as does the U.K. in **Bark (bark.com)**.

Thumbtack (thumbtack.com)—Not entirely dissimilar to Task-Rabbit, Thumbtack allows you to offer a broader spectrum of services, from photography to singing lessons, tutoring, locksmithing, and cooking. The business model is slightly different in that buyers submit a brief/request and service providers pay a nominal fee to bid for the job. The bidding process isn't too overcrowded, though, with a limit on the number of bidders per job.

Are You a Natural Coach?

If your calling is life coaching, like mine, you will understand that getting exposure and attracting new clients can be pretty tough when starting out. Fortunately there are a couple of platforms dedicated to those looking to coach and teach.

Noomii (noomii.com)—According to the site, they are the web's largest directory of life coaches and business coaches. Potential clients describe their goals and are matched with a coach based on suitability. After the coach and the client have a free 15-minute consult, they can decide whether they want to continue.

Coach.me (coach.me)—Also a life and business coaching database. Members pay an annual fee, but this is refunded if you don't earn that back from business garnered through the site.

Udemy (udemy.com)—A huge online education marketplace that allows you to teach online courses from anywhere in the world. It currently has 20,000 instructors and eleven million students, is located in 190 countries, and has average instructor earnings of $8,000. Courses on offer cover a wide variety of options, from music to design, marketing, personal development, health and fitness, language, test prep, IT and software, and more. Udemy also provides useful tools to help you create your course in a format that is a fit for their platform.

CoachUp (coachup.com)—Are you a former sports star, looking to give back to the game that brought you so much joy? This may be a great place for you to offer your services. CoachUp allows you to offer private coaching and team sports training in more than 30 sports. You get to decide on your rate and schedule. My husband loves basketball; a quick look at basketball coaches in our area shows me they are charging anywhere from $50 to $130 per session.

Are You a Trusty Assistant?

I used to be a recruitment consultant that worked with C-level executives to hire world-class executive assistants, and I can tell you, being a reliable assistant is a true skill. It could also make for a great side hustle, and there are quite a few platforms that allow you to let busy people know that you are happy to run errands for them, for a price!

Hello Alfred (helloalfred.com)—You can earn up to $25 an hour for running errands as simple as picking up/delivering laundry, grocery shopping/fridge restocking, housecleaning, tailoring or shoe repair, sorting mail, picking up prescription medication, delivering packages, and more.

WeGoLook (wegolook.com)—I found this one to be very interesting. According to their site, you can earn $25–$200/hour performing tasks such as inspections of autos, auction items, property, and more. Get paid to check them out, send photos, and report back with the details. A friend of ours was looking to buy an investment property down in Charlotte while living in Chicago. Flying back and forth to look at properties would obviously be expensive, so a solution like this (without the bias of a real estate broker) may be a great solution.

My List of Resources

Now that you've selected the right side hustle, you may need to get help as you set it up. The resources below are all ones that I either have used myself or have heard about through the positive experiences of friends. My suggestion would be to research each (as well as others) to see what would be the best fit for your business and financial goals/situation. This should act as a nice starting point as you start to plan your next steps.

Website/Blogging Design Platforms

WordPress—My current website was built by my designer using WordPress. It is a very user-friendly platform and relatively intuitive, so after the initial setup you should be able to make any minor changes on your own (with perhaps a little help from Google). Many of the most popular blogs were built using WordPress.

Squarespace

Disqus—This is a fantastic commenting tool/plug-in that I have seen on many of the more popular blogs and comment-enabled sites. I used it on mine.

Domain Name Registrars

GoDaddy
HostGator

One thing to note is that when you buy your domain, you want to find out whether or not the domain is being hosted on a shared server. This is critical for when traffic to your site increases. As traffic to my site grew, I had issues with my site taking a long time to load due to the fact that it was being hosted on a shared server. I then had it moved to a virtual private server (VPS).

Email/CRM Tools

MailChimp—I used MailChimp when I first started and really liked it because it was free up to a certain level of subscribers.

Ontraport—Once my business started to scale, I switched to Ontraport, as I found it to be a better all-in-one platform for email and product launch management. It isn't cheap, though, and costs me around $300/month.

Infusionsoft—I was initially leaning towards Infusionsoft when I switched from MailChimp, but decided to go with Ontraport because I felt it was a better fit for my business. Do your homework, though. A lot of really successful people use Infusionsoft and find it to be a better fit for them.

ConvertKit—another CRM platform worth checking out.

Payment Processors

PayPal
Square
Venmo

Virtual Assistant Services

Fiverr
Brickwork India
YourManInIndia

Creative Services

99designs
Fiverr—(again! Notice a pattern?)
Vistaprint—for your business cards, launch party invites, and more

Online Webinar/Teleseminar Services

FreeConferenceCall.com
GoToWebinar
WebinarJam

Legal

I would strongly suggest consulting with a lawyer before setting up shop. Many will do a free consultation, from which you can get a lot of valuable information in terms of the type of legal structure you should set up and ongoing requirements. For a cheaper alternative (and one that I used to set my business up) you may want to look at a company like LegalZoom to help with the legal side at a relatively affordable price. This could cover liability, taxes, local certification requirements, or trademark issues. Each business will have its own unique considerations—don't get blindsided!

Accounting

Choose an accountant who really knows what your business is about. Get a local referral if you can! A good accountant will help you maximize the profitability of your business while adhering to any taxation and reporting requirements. I went through a number of accountants before finding one I felt comfortable with. In the last year or so I also hired a bookkeeper. She can do in one hour what would take me much longer, so I was happy to pay $70/hour so I could focus on growing revenue. She also has a close working relationship with my accountant, which is ideal.

My Favorite Inspirational Resources

This book not enough for you? Read on!

Books

Choose Yourself!—James Altucher
The Life-Changing Magic of Tidying Up—Marie Kondo

The Magic of Thinking Big—David Schwartz

The Little Red Book of Selling—Jeffrey Gitomer

Feel the Fear . . . and Do It Anyway—Susan Jeffers

The Success Principles—Jack Canfield

Life Loves You—Louise Hay

Steal Like an Artist—Austin Kleon

Do the Work—Steven Pressfield

The Law of Divine Compensation—Marianne Williamson

The 4-Hour Workweek—Tim Ferriss

The Art of Non-Conformity—Chris Guillebeau

Get Rich, Lucky Bitch!—Denise Duffield-Thomas

Plus: Biographies of anyone who inspires you.

Podcasts

The James Altucher Show

James is a hedge-fund manager and entrepreneur who wrote one of my favorite books, *Choose Yourself!*

Tara Brach

A psychotherapist and meditation teacher, Tara founded the Insight Meditation Community.

The Charged Life with Brendon Burchard

A best-selling author, Brendon dispenses tips on motivation, success, high performance, and otherwise living a fully charged life.

The RobCast by Rob Bell

A former pastor, Rob shares the insights that have made

him a guest on Oprah's SuperSoul Sessions.

Being Boss Podcast

This podcast is run by a community of creative entrepreneurs dedicated to the state of mind that is boss life.

This Is Your Life Podcast with Michael Hyatt

Best-selling author Michael Hyatt focuses his podcast on intentional leadership.

Magic Lessons with Elizabeth Gilbert

Elizabeth Gilbert guides readers to express their creativity and live more authentically.

Dr. Wayne W. Dyer Podcast

On this show, Dr. Dyer answered questions from listeners on how to deal with life's challenges, personal and professional.

The Tim Ferriss Show

Productivity guru Tim Ferriss invites on world-class performers from areas such as investing, chess, pro sports, and more to find the tools, tactics, and tricks from their success that listeners can use.

Acknowledgments

A big thank-you to Greatist, Business Insider, Huffington Post, News.com.au, and Hearst, who allowed me to use parts of my published articles in this book.

An extra-special thanks to Nora Rawn, Heath Collins, Hannah Tattersall, Locke Hughes, Rysia Trembeth, and every single kick-ass interviewee in this book, for making it all possible.

> *"There comes a special moment in everyone's life, a moment for which that person was born. . . . When he seizes it . . . It is his finest hour."*
> –Winston Churchill